DEFINING MOMENT

DEFINING MOMENT

Motivating People To Take Action

Brent Filson

Williamstown, Massachusetts 1993

Magalis:
This book is not for you; it is you — and from you, us: to live what we spoke at High Hollow.

Printed in the United States of America

Grateful acknowledgment is made for the right to reprint "How Not to Make a Speech in Japan" by Brent Filson from Leaders April/May/June 1992 issue.

ISBN 0-9626845-5-4

Published by Williamstown Publishing Company P.O. Box 295
Williamstown, MA 01267

CONTENTS

3. BELIEF 21

4. THE DEFINING MOMENT 37

5. CHARACTERISTICS OF THE DEFINING MOMENT 53

9. ACTION FROM VISION 103

10. THE CALL TO ACTION 119

11. HUMOR 131

12. DELIVERY 149

13. THE GLOBAL ACTION LEADER 179

14. THE SPEECH BEGINS AFTER THE SPEECH IS FINISHED 187

PREFACE

A crisis of leadership afflicts our nation. Unions and management view each other as enemies. Business leaders fatten their salaries and pensions while laying off workers. Politicians and voters distrust and scorn each other. Supervisors and employees engage in feeding frenzies for power perks. The result: Though we must compete in the global economic wars, we are fighting a civil war.

Clearly, leadership is vital to business success. Every failure in business is ultimately human failure, every success human success. Just as the Vermont preacher said, "if you see somebody sleeping in my congregation, march right up and wake . . . me; wake me, the preacher. I'm responsible!" so the leaders are responsible for the failure or success of people they lead.

But a fundamental misunderstanding about leadership pervades our country. Many believe that leadership involves giving orders. But today new business realities are requiring the development and execution of new kinds of leadership, leadership that has very little to do with order giving.

Since the beginning of the Industrial Revolution, the order-giving way of leadership has flourished. *Order* comes from a Latin root meaning to arrange threads in a woof. In the Revolution's early years, captains of industry dealt with the relatively uneducated country people in their factories by ordering them where, how and when to work. The most efficient and effective production methods were created when workers were "ordered" or ranked like threads in the woof of production lines. Refined and empowered by the Victorian culture, with its patriarchal power structure and strong links to Prussian military organization and dictates, the culture of the order-giver leader reached its zenith in the United States after World War II.

In the following two or three decades, with most of the industrialized world recovering from the war, many U.S. businesses were like majestic ocean liners plowing through relatively calm seas, their leaders, like liner captains and mates, running things by getting orders from superiors, giving orders to subordinates, and making sure those orders were carried out. But we know that businesses around the world are undergoing changes as radical as any since the beginning of the Industrial Revolution. With competition increasing dramatically, with the volume and velocity of information multiplying, with information becoming accessible to more and more people, with the traditional, pyramidal structures of order-giving businesses flattening, leaders today need skills akin not to ocean liner piloting but white-water canoeing. Order leadership founders in an environment where the lines of authority are blurred, information widely disseminated, markets rapidly changing, and employees are empowered. In such an environment, new leadership is needed.

My experience as an infantry officer, as a journalist who has interviewed more than 2,000 people, as a business owner and consultant who has worked closely with some of the most successful leaders in the United States and Europe, has convinced me that this new leadership will come from people who do not give orders so much as they motivate people to take action. And they do that by establishing a rich *emotional* relationship with the people they lead.

Motivation... *emotion*... *motion*... they derive from the same Latin word meaning "to move." When you want to motivate people to move, engage their emotions. Become not an order leader but an "action leader."

This book will help you become that kind of leader. It is a call to action and a plan for action that you can put into action right away and in your own way help turn the crisis of leadership into a golden age of leadership.

ACKNOWLEDGEMENT

OFTEN, I DON'T write words, words write me. This book was written before it was ever set to words. It was written when the publication of *Executive Speeches* gave me the opportunity to speak to many people across the nation: to leaders in board rooms, people on picket lines and assembly lines, students, talk show hosts and listeners, seminar audiences, politicians and voters, managers and general managers, supervisors and reporters.

Throughout my travels, I realized that a book was being pounded out in the crucible of those exchanges, a sequel to *Executive Speeches* that would help people turn the historic changes taking place in business today to their advantage. So here's to the many people that helped shape the amalgam, people whose heartfelt responses to action leadership helped produce a defining moment for me, the moment that motivated me to tip the crucible over and let this book pour out.

INTRODUCTION

THIS BOOK IS not a quick read. It is meant to be used throughout your career. But you can put the book to use right away. Go to the last page of Chapter 1. Read the three questions. Apply them when you need to motivate people to take action. If you answer "no" to any one of the questions, don't speak. However, don't let the questions be a barrier to speaking. Leaders do nothing more important than motivate people to take action, and speech is a key trigger of that motivation. Make the questions be a springboard to your motivational speech. Reflect upon them until you can answer "yes" to each one. Then speak.

Action leadership isn't a system of techniques; instead, it is a way of living, a lifelong journey into the hearts of the people you relate to and also into your heart. You'll never get it right — and that's the good news! As an action leader, get used to living by the code, *Absolutum obsoletum* : If it works it's out of date.

Yet though the meaning of the motivational relationship is found in action and ambiguity (without ambiguity there would be no freedom to take action), *that relationship must, paradoxically, work; it must get results in the marketplace.* Action leaders must replace order leaders for no other reason than the fact that action leadership succeeds.

Replacing order leadership with action leadership is not a change in degree but in kind. Throughout history new tools shaped evolutions in the way things were made and used, but new materials shaped revolutions. It's no accident that the epochs of civilization are divided by materials: stone, copper, bronze, etc., because it is not refinement but *changes in materials* that create fundamental advancements in civilizations. As with materials, the greatest advancements in leadership will happen not when we refine order-giving techniques, but when we change materials, as it were, when we become new leaders by becoming action leaders.

This doesn't mean that if you have been an order leader, you will be consigned to the scrap heap of business history. On the contrary, you possess the key ingredient of action leadership: defining moments. This book will help you make those moments live in the hearts of the people you lead and thus transform your dream of leadership, through them, into action and results.

DEFINING MOMENT:
Motivating People to Take Action

1

Motivation: A Raving Cliché

BUSINESS IS ACTION. Employees must act to develop, produce and sell products and services. Customers must act to buy them. People act only when moved or motivated to act. Yet motivation in business has become a raving cliché of our age, mainly because many leaders don't understand who motivates whom.

Businesses hire speakers to deliver "motivational" speeches to their employees; sales and marketing executives develop motivational strategies and modules; and advertisers create ads to motivate customers to buy — under the assumption that people can be motivated. Horsefeathers!

That false assumption leads to the dog-track mentality of leadership. Create a fake rabbit that keeps people running in safe circles and call it motivation. Call it leadership. The truth is, nobody can motivate anybody to do anything. Motivation doesn't start with so-called motivators. It starts with the *motivatees.* People are only motivated when they motivate themselves. To cultivate the art of motivating people to take action, understand that *the motivator and the motivatee are always the same person.* Communication is what you do. Motivation is what they do. The motivational speech isn't a thing you deliver to people, but a dance you do with them.

"WE DANCE"

A European theologian asked a Japanese Zen master, "Your religion has no canons, no scriptures. What do you have?"

"Nothing," said the master. "We just dance."

An all-star major league shortstop, known for his acrobatic moves, said, "My secret is that I make the ball my dance partner."

The dance is the metaphor of motivational speech because such speech often has the spontaneity and grace of a one-motion-backhand-stab-in-the-hole-and-rifle-throw-to-first — all the result of practice and hard work.

NOT ACTION, RESULTS

There's another misunderstanding about motivation. Many leaders think that motivation is an end in itself. Motivation is not an end, it is the means to the end. That end is results. Motivated people are not valuable to a business. People who simply take action are not valuable to a business. Only people who get results are valuable. But motivated people who take action have the best chance of getting results.

EXPAND THE CONTEXT

Motivation most often happens through speech. But we must expand the context of the motivational speech. I'm talking about formal speeches you might give before large groups of people and also the many informal speeches you must give every day.

When trying to argue a cop out of a traffic ticket, you must give a motivational speech.

When grounding your teen-ager, you must give a motivational speech.

When applying for a job or a promotion and the person on the other side of the desk asks, "How can you contribute?", you must give a motivational speech.

We give speeches every day. And the techniques for the formal and informal speech are identical.

THE SPEECH IS NOT A PRESENTATION

One more thing: The motivational speech is *not* a presentation.

The function of a presentation is to communicate information.

The function of a speech is to motivate people to take action.

The presentation appeals to reason.

The speech makes fannies squirm, figuratively or literally.

Harry Cohen, one-time head of Columbia Pictures, gives the literal example. He said that he had a foolproof means for determining a movie's value. "When I'm watching it, if my fanny squirms, it's a good picture. If my fanny doesn't squirm, it's a bad picture."

If your audience's fannies aren't in some way squirming, you are not giving a motivational speech.

THE EMOTIONAL CONNECTION

To engage in a dance of motivation with an audience — whether two or 2,000 people — you must establish an emotional connection with that audience.

A few years after delivering his secret speech denouncing Stalin, Soviet Prime Minister Nikita Khrushchev was speaking at a meeting of Communist Party officials when somebody in the back of the room shouted, "You were Stalin's colleague; why didn't you say something, why didn't you do something?"

Khrushchev glared at the audience and roared, "WHO SAID THAT?"

The audience sat there, silent, quailing in their chairs. Then Khrushchev said quietly, "Now you know why I said nothing. Now you know why I did nothing."

In responding, Khrushchev did not give a presentation. He did not communicate information. Instead, he gave, in those brief moments, a speech. He argued his case by making their fannies squirm.

SILENCE, THE BEST SPEECH

The difference between success and failure in motivating people to take action often hinges on leaving things unsaid. Too many business leaders say the wrong things at the wrong time. Just as the best part of a manufactured product is that part which is eliminated — in reality a "no part" — so the best speech is "no speech." "Heard melodies," said the poet John Keats, "are sweet. But those unheard are sweetest." The Cheyenne saying, "Have less thunder in the mouth and more lightning in the hand," recognizes that we damage ourselves more by what comes out of our mouths than what our rivals and competitors ever do.

So don't speak unless you can improve upon the silence. The saying that "the journey of 1,000 miles begins with the first step" is less discerning than "the journey is over before you raise your foot."

set your blocks before speaking

Just as you yourself are the journey and encompass its beginning, middle and end in this moment, so you are the speech before you speak. You, without words, are the most powerful motivating factor of all.

A sprinting champion said, "A 100-yard dash begins not when I start running, but when I set my blocks. A quick start and powering up quickly to top speed isn't a matter of pushing hard out of the blocks; it's a matter of getting those blocks set properly so that my arms and legs have correct angles just before the gun goes off."

Before you give your motivational speech, set your blocks properly by asking three questions. If you answer "no" to any one of these questions, don't speak.

THREE TRIGGERS OF MOTIVATION

— Do I know what the audience needs?
— Do I believe in what I'm saying?
— Can I have that audience take action?

Don't speak until you can say "yes" to all the questions.

Let's examine the triggers and how you can put them into use right now.

2

Audience Need

THE FOCUS OF motivational speech is not you, the speaker, but your audience. Without an audience there is no speech. I bring you this BFO, this Blinding Flash of the Obvious, because too many speakers forget this point. One observer's description of the United States Congress that, "someone gets up, speaks and says nothing; people hear but nobody listens; then everybody disagrees," can also describe the interplay so many leaders have with their audiences. After all, you might be speaking to 1,000 people, but if no one is listening, you have, in point of fact, no audience at all. The remarkable thing about Boris Yeltsin delivering his famous, defiant speech atop a tank in August 1991 was not only that he was facing down the armed might of Communist reactionaries with nothing more than words spoken from scribbled notes, but that nobody pulled the plug. For whatever reasons, the coup leaders did not shut down television coverage. Boris Yeltsin had a worldwide audience. Mikhail Gorbachev, held captive in his Black Sea *dacha*, gave an impassioned speech — to a video recorder. The speech wasn't aired. Gorbachev didn't have an audience. History was changed by the man who had an audience.

THE ART OF SERVING

The people you lead only listen when they want to hear. A key way to get them to listen is to serve them. As a leader, you have power over others. Some leaders think that they aren't leading well unless they use that power, and blood must be mopped from the walls. But as Robert E. Lee said, "Those who have power over others should forbear using it. A true man of honor humbles himself when he cannot help humbling others."

Pericles' greatest achievement

When the Athenian general and statesman Pericles lay dying of the plague that ravished Athens for several years during the Peloponnesian War, his companions gathered beside his deathbed and spoke to one another of the many military victories he had brought Athens. Pericles seemed to be unconscious. However, all the while he had been listening and finally spoke up and said that his military triumphs were far less important than what he considered his greatest achievement: "That no Athenian, through my means, ever wore mourning." After Pericles' death, the Athenians quickly felt his loss. As Plutarch said, "Those who, while he lived, resented his great authority, as that which eclipsed themselves, presently after his quitting the stage, making trial of other orators and demagogues, readily acknowledged that there never had been in nature such a disposition as his was, more moderate and reasonable in height of that state he took upon him, or grave and impressive in the mildness that he displayed."

leadership is service

Since action leadership isn't a function of power but of service, the more you give of yourself to the people you lead, the more you get from them. When you do not demand action from people but instead serve them so they might act from their own motives, you will be speaking to people who want to hear.

EASY IS HARD

I do not mean that in serving your audience, you become servile and/or try to make things easy for that audience. Motivating your audience often means challenging them to undertake great difficulties. They will love you for it. Just as great salesmanship has little regard for price, great action leadership has little regard for difficulties.

As Thoreau recognized in *Walden*, "I have traveled a good deal in Concord; and everywhere, in shops, and offices, and fields, the inhabitants have appeared to me to be doing penance in a thousand remarkable ways. What I have heard of Brahmins sitting exposed to four fires and looking in the face of the sun; or hanging suspended, with their heads downward, over flames; or looking at three heavens over their shoulders until it becomes impossible for them to resume their natural position, while from the twist of the neck nothing but liquids can pass into the stomach; or dwelling, chained for life, at the foot of a tree; or measuring with their bodies like caterpillars, the breadth of vast empires; or standing on one leg on tops of pillars — even these forms of conscious penance are hardly more incredible and astonishing than the scenes which I daily witness. The twelve labors of Hercules were trifling in comparison with those which my neighbors have undertaken; for they were only twelve and had an end but I could never see that these men slew or captured any monster or finished any labor. . . How many a poor immortal soul have I met well-nigh crushed and smothered under its load, creeping down the road of life, pushing before it a barn seventy-five feet by forty, its Augean stables never cleansed, and one hundred acres of land, tillage, mowing, pasture and wood-lot!"

relax and have fun

Thoreau is right about the extraordinary labors humans will undertake to further their self interest, but the people you lead should not be "poor souls" crushed by work. If they and you aren't having fun in your work, you may be screwing up. I'm not saying that you should not be serious about your work. But leaders who can't find joy even in serious activities are disadvantaged. Take the advice of many athletes who perform well under pressure: They testify that they do best when, at the moment of execution, whether running, skating, batting, pitching, etc., they relax and have fun.

Since, for many people, the hard way is the easy way, action leaders need not worry that their audiences might not be up to the task, however improbable or even impossible it might seem; what must concern action leaders is that the impulse to act comes from the audiences themselves. People might obey orders from an order leader and simply get a specific job done and nothing more; but they will happily come in to work in the dark and go out in the dark when they motivate themselves. As the man said, trying to run faster when being chased by a bear, "Lord, you pick 'em up, and I'll lay' em down!"

AUDIENCE NEED

The most important way to serve your audience is to answer their needs. Motivation springs from needs. I say needs, not wants. To motivate people, don't ask what your audience wants, ask what they need. It is indispensable to our happiness that we do not often get what we want. Getting half our wants could very well double our troubles. But striving to get what we need is the gateway to freedom of action.

Knowing the difference between audience wants and needs is

a key goal of action leadership. Often the audience themselves cannot distinguish between their wants and their needs. But as an action leader, you must.

Here are eight ways to make that distinction.

1. NEED IS THE MAJOR PROBLEM

In business, security is peril. As in physics, mass and energy are different manifestations of the same substance, so in business, security and peril are the interchangeable manifestations of need. If your customers are not in peril, they would not have needs. If they did not have needs, you would have no business. "We need problems to progress," said Charles F. Kettering. "Don't bring me anything but trouble!"

Wants and needs differ both in kind and in degree. A want is a minor problem of an audience. A need is a major problem of that audience. Ask, "What is the most important problem facing my audience?", and you begin to understand not what they want but what they need.

2. NEED IS A HUMAN BEING

Business isn't operated by the numbers but by the people. View a want in terms of a human being, and you have often transformed that want into a need. Don't ask, who does your audience want to hear? Ask instead, *who do they need to hear?* Who is the most important person that can speak to the audience?

Great motivational speeches have been made by speakers who were transformed, often during the speech, in the audience's estimation from somebody they wanted to hear into somebody they needed to hear.

In fact, that very transformation is often a powerful motivational technique.

the joke general

During World War II's North African campaign when Erwin Rommel's brigades were rolling up the Allied forces and seemed headed for inevitable victory, a brilliant general was selected to take over the beleaguered and demoralized British army. However, on the way to his field headquarters, the general was killed in a plane crash. The second-choice general left a staff job in England and made a hasty flight to Cairo then rode into the desert to the Eighth Army headquarters. Climbing out of his car, he ordered his staff to assemble around him. Battle-weary, sun-browned, and demoralized, the soldiers gathered about the thin-faced, hawk-nosed general, who had never before been in the desert, his untanned, skinny limbs sticking awkwardly out of a new uniform.

a turnaround speech

He got up on an ammunition crate and proceeded to give a speech. He told them that the Eighth Army was no longer going to retreat, that they were going to fight where they stood, that when Rommel attacked, they would beat him to a standstill, then *they* would go on the attack and "hit Rommel for six right out of Africa." An officer who heard that speech said that the men thought he was a joke-general when he got up on that crate to speak. "But at the end of that marvelous speech," the officer recalls, "We knew that the new commanding officer, Field Marshal 'Monty' Montgomery, was *our* general, and that we began to feel that we could win."

white knees

Nearly two decades later, Montgomery himself wrote about that speech and recalled that his talk was received in complete silence. "But it certainly had a profound effect and a spirit of hope, anyway of clarity, was born that evening; one thing was very clear to the staff: There was to be no more uncertainty about anything. But the old hands thought that my knees were very white!"

3. NEED IS ACTION

If an audience simply wants something, they can bide their time getting it. But if an audience needs something, they urgently want to take action.

Ask what your audience must urgently do. That is what they need.

4. NEED IS FEELING

The end of every motivational speech is action. Yet often, an audience must *feel* in order to act. A want generates a fragile emotion. But a need creates strong feelings that can trigger decisive actions.

Ask what the audience needs to feel before they can act.

For instance, many audiences need to feel that they can know and trust the person with whom they dance.

Montgomery's speech struck a responsive chord in his audience because their need to trust in his mettle was strong.

When he spoke words that transformed him in their estimation from a donkey of a staff officer to a lion of a leader, tying into their need to believe in him and trust him, then a member of his audience could truly say that he was "our" general and that even in retreat, they could begin to think and act like victorious soldiers.

5. NEED IS ANGER

Determine what your audience needs by asking what makes them angry. A person angry is a person who feels wronged. The gauge of their need is the measure of that perceived wrong. To make an emotional connection with people, don't take the teeth out of emotions. Don't bottle up emotions. ("My problem is that I never get angry," said Woody Allen. "I grow a tumor instead.") And don't have your audience bottle anger up.

As a leader you will face many angry audiences. Use anger. Dance with it. After all, you're facing a strong need in the guise of a perceived wrong. Anger is a bucking bronco. Straddle your fear of other people's anger, jerk the cinch and ride. It's better to get bucked off and go sprawling under bright lights than sit in the stall stewing uselessly. Keep with it, and you'll learn much about your audience and even more about yourself.

angry work force

I know of a CEO of a manufacturing firm who was fired only two years after he was given the job, and he still doesn't know why. He thought he had done everything right in trying to turn a company around. He had streamlined the work force, improved productivity, made the company more customer-responsive and improved product margins by cutting costs. Yet despite its being dressed up in traditional turnaround raiment, the company remained mired in red ink. The reason: He had angered the employees. His best employees left the company, and the mediocre ones just pretended to work.

Angering people wasn't his mistake. Most leaders get people angry at them many times. Yet good leaders can still lead angry people to achieve great successes. The CEO made his fatal mistake because he simply did not get out and see the people he had angered.

get out and see the people

"Get out and see the people" is the sine qua non of the

motivational speech. I worked with the owner of an enormously successful medical device manufacturing firm. He began his career as a high school dropout working on an assembly line.

He said that there are three rules in business: "Get out and see the people. Get out and see the people. Get out and see the people."

He also said: "I've never given a formal speech in my life — though I must give 20-to-25 informal speeches every day." In other words, he never delivered a formal communication behind a podium to an audience. Knowing that you cannot motivate from memos and monitors, he was always out with the people, interacting personally with them.

a strategy of being cooped up

One leader succeeded. The other failed. Why?

The CEO did not get out and see the people and give 20-to-25 speeches a day. Instead, he remained cooped up in his office, working the levers of his elegant, polished strategy, not knowing that strategy isn't only what you plan but what people do.

persuade with your ears

Seeing the people is not enough. When you see them, talk to them. Or more important: Have them talk to you. Persuade with your ears, by listening to people. Ask, "What specifically do you want changed immediately?" Or: "How can I help you do your job better?" Or: "In a year from now, what do you want this job to be?" Or, sometimes more important, ask about their families, find out if they have personal problems, try to help them with their problems. Remember the names of their family members and their particular needs.

"Hello, Herb!"

A president of a major materials company in Asia was stationed on an aircraft carrier 30 years ago and still remembers a moment that took place between the carrier's captain and him. "I was a lowly ensign, and the captain had just reported for duty on the carrier, which was manned by several thousand sailors and Marines. At a rather formal welcoming ceremony, I was one of a long line of officers introduced to him. He shook my hand then went on to the next officer. About a week later, we passed each other in some far-off corner of the carrier. He said, 'Hello, Herb!' What a thrill I got. He had only met me briefly when I was one of scores of officers in a receiving line, yet seeing me a week later, he remembered me *and* my name. I've never forgotten that. Throughout my career, I've made it a point of remembering the names and the concerns of *all* the people I lead."

The challenge of action leadership often isn't to get people to do what they want to do — it's to get people to do what they *don't* want to do and like it. When you serve people by being genuinely concerned for them, you'll often get them liking what they are doing even though they may not want to do it.

6. NEED IS FEAR

What an audience fears it also needs. Fear and need are two sides of the same coin. Flip the fear and there's the need.

Fear: I'm going to lose my job. Need: I must keep my job. Fear: The competition will win the contract. Need: I need this contract. Fear: We are going out of business. Need: We must save this business!

It's a simple technique, changing fears into needs, but it's a technique that must be accomplished with practically every motivational speech, so people are motivated to trust their hopes, not their fears.

the crack cocaine of leadership

Clearly, fear is a powerful motivator. A good scare can be great advice. Fear has force, but what about direction? A reindeer herd, spooked by fear, rushing first one way then another, is clearly motivated, but is it going anywhere?

Love, it is said, conquers all. But one wonders what was conquered through love by Peter the Great when he tried to motivate his mistress to remain faithful by having her lover decapitated and displaying the head in a jar of alcohol beside her bed. Fear is the crack cocaine of leadership, easy to use for a quick fix, but habit forming and enslaving. As you measure slaves' freedom by the lengths of their chains, so you measure fearful people's motivation by the cramped spaces of their fears.

fear begets fears

Fear begets fears. Many people living in the former Communist countries will be struggling with the psychological legacy of rule-by-fear for the rest of their lives.

For instance, a political leader in Poland, a Solidarity stalwart, said that after the overthrow of Communism, he still is ruled by fears. "The fear of risks," he says, "The fear of something new, the fear of competition."

A good leader inspires people to have confidence in her. A great leader inspires people to have confidence in themselves. Fear pulls up that confidence, root and branch.

7. NEED IS DREAMS

Dreams as well as facts motivate people to take action. I'm not talking about sleeping dreams, but waking dreams ("Hope," said Aristotle, "is a waking dream."), those dreams in which we see the invisible, feel the intangible, and do what may seem impossible.

Dreams are a kind of internal action that lead to powerful external action. Every great business was once a dream in one person's heart. A great leader inspires an audience to dream that they themselves can become great. Leaders and the people they lead must dream together to dance together, though clearly we cannot dream our way to success, but must hammer and forge that success.

Ask what an audience dreams (i.e., what do they fervently hope will come to pass?), and your answer is a powerful need.

8. NEED IS LOVE

To many people, love has as much place in business as chocolate syrup on a porterhouse steak. With sexual harassment being such a prominent issue, many leaders wouldn't get caught dead committing a flagrant act of love in their business dealings.

Yet if the dance of motivation is essentially an emotional dance, then how can we eliminate that powerful motivator, love? Not love manifested through sexual attraction, but agape love born of a deep desire to serve a person or a cause.

If leadership is service then why can't love be an ultimate function of motivation? Often in the Marine Corps I heard the word *love* expressed within the context of leadership. Time and again great leaders were described this way: "The troops love him. They would follow him into hell with water buckets."

Every person I have known in and out of the military who said they truly loved their leader, spoke with pride and deep emotion that beckoned like a liberation.

ACTION TO TAKE:

Motivational speech is about fact and faith. It's a fact that you're speaking, but it's faith that you are communicating. That fact/faith gap narrows when you speak to and fulfill their needs.

— Understand that before you speak, you must know what your audience needs. You can only motivate people to take action when you are the embodiment of the answer to their needs.

— Find their need by transforming into questions the eight techniques for distinguishing a want from a need. Ask: 1. What is their major problem? 2. Who do they need to have speak to them? 3. What action do they need to take? 4. What do they need to feel? 5. What do they need to feel angry about? 6. What do they need to fear? 7. What do they need to dream about? 8. Who or what do they need to love?

— Boil your answers down to a single, compelling need. It could be any one of the eight answers or a combination of several of them. A great salesman told me, "Always sell only one thing at a time." That is true with motivational speeches. Each speech should speak to just a few needs.

— *Feel* those needs. Knowledge comes from the mind and the heart. "Anybody who has a bull by the tail," said Mark Twain, "knows about five or six things more than somebody who hasn't." Grab the bull of the audience by the tail by feeling what they feel. When you speak, their fear, anger, or love must be your fear, anger or love. If they're not, don't speak.

— Take care that your speaking to their needs doesn't make you swell but makes you grow instead. The essence of action leadership lies in the opportunities you give to others, not in the opportunities they may give to you. Approach your audience not with a puffed-up ego but with the attitude that their needs are always more important than yours.

3

Belief

IN GRAND OPERA, you can do anything as long as you sing it. With motivational speech, you can do nothing unless you and your audience feel it. Feelings, not just words and facts, motivate people to act. The Irish saying, "seeing is believing, but feeling is God's own truth," is the motivational speech's credo.

Your audience won't get the feelings you want them to get unless you yourself get them first. Conviction is the engine of action leadership. Without your bringing a kind of religious devotion to the dance, it won't take place, or at least won't be done well.

Before speaking, ask: Do I absolutely believe in what I'm saying?

If the answer is "no," don't speak.

The next three chapters will help you answer "yes!"

To get the best out of people, go to the best in yourself — and in them. Before we get to the best in you, your defining moment, here are six ways to enable you to say what you feel and feel what you say.

1. TRUST EMOTION

Telling many order leaders to trust their emotions in business situations is like asking them to line up for mass spinal taps. The culture of order leadership does not require dealing with emotions, let alone trusting them — though blowing one's stack (a quick temper being many an order leader's peacock hat) is condoned since it involves using emotion not as a helping hand but as a club. One simply gives an order, goes away and maybe comes back later to see if the order is being carried out. Feeling and communicating that feeling are irrelevant, stupid or embarrassing — or all three. But in action leadership, emotion is the music of the dance.

two paths to knowledge

Throughout history, humans have, in general, walked two paths to knowledge, the path of reason and the path of experience. To a large extent, our culture, so dependent on science and technology, has been shaped by rational knowledge. That influence has been clearly felt in business. Order leadership is systematically rational. So are most manufacturing and service methodologies. For instance, during the past several decades, businesses have enhanced the quality of their products and manufacturing processes through quantitative analysis. Their leaders have been successful at describing and shaping quality not by hunches or subjective experience but by charts, graphs, diagrams and other tools of mass data. They have made quality measurable and repeatable. But there is another quality dynamic: That's the quality of leadership. That quality cannot be number-described or number-driven. Instead, it is a quality of *communicated emotion.* That is based on rational knowledge but also, to a large degree, on experiential knowledge.

experiential knowledge

Because we look at the world through the lens of our rational culture, we often miss the importance of experiential knowledge. In many tribal cultures, experiential knowledge — deriving from dreams, dancing, rites-of-passage rituals, etc. — is considered sublime knowledge. In addition, Asian religions, Buddhism for instance, view the seat of reason, the intellect, as merely a side show to the main show which is the vast unconscious. One objective of meditation is to still the workings of the intellect, or the "monkey mind" as the Hindus call it, so that the meditator can think and act spontaneously from the fountains of the subconscious. The sages of Asia asserted that true knowledge is acquired by experiencing the moment at hand. Knowledge then is thought and action. More important, it's thought in action. For the sages, the knowledge born of intellect segments reality, but knowledge born of experience makes reality whole.

production and philosophy

As to our advancements in quality: Success can breed bad habits and bad ideas. Because intellectual knowledge (the quantification of quality) has been so successful, the application of experiential knowledge to leadership has been greatly neglected. "Productivity increases as variability decreases," said W. Edwards Deming, a pioneer in integrating statistical quality control (SQC) with manufacturing processes. He described both production and philosophical values. But often the effectiveness of action leadership increases as variability and subjectivity not decrease but increase. Action leadership thrives on experiential knowledge, on surprise, diversity and paradox, on two plus two not always equaling four. As Winston Churchill said, in regard to leading people, "Sometimes two plus two equals five or six. The blackboard gets knocked over. The teacher gets a black eye. And the class is in turmoil!"

not a prison break

I'm not advocating our creating an action-leadership environment like a prison break. But if we, in our quest to quantify quality, give ourselves over totally to intellect and fail to come to grips with the emotional dimensions of business and leadership, then in today's time of great global change, we fail the people we lead, our businesses and ourselves.

emotion and business

Let's face it, business is fundamentally an emotional activity.

Charles Dickens' observation in *David Copperfield* that "Annual income twenty pounds, annual expenditure nineteen nineteen, six, result happiness. Annual income twenty pounds, annual expenditure twenty pounds ought and six, result misery," applies in principle to mom-and-pop stores as well as international conglomerates.

2. FEEL THE EMOTION OF THE OCCASION

But trusting your emotions is only a first step. You must put that trust into action. You must not only see the speaking occasion but *feel* it as well.

Every motivational speech is grounded in the drama of the occasion. Drama is conflict. Conflict generates emotion. Analyze the drama by asking, "What conflict is taking place? What emotion is there?" See the drama and emotion in every occasion and make every occasion an opportunity for the communication of that drama and emotion.

Is your business losing market share? Is your business changing management? Is your technology going through a middle-age crisis? Are foreign competitors at the gates? Are your best people going out the exit doors? Drama and emotion pervade these occurrences.

Know what the audience needs *and* what is at stake. That question, "What is at stake?" is where you often find the emotion.

What's at stake means what is important about the need. A sales force might need to make $500,000 this quarter. But only when you know what's at stake — i.e., the business will close if they don't make the numbers — will you know the depth of emotion involved.

Seize the occasion by feeling the drama of what's at stake. That feeling is the conviction from which you speak.

3. RAISE THE STAKES

John Donne wrote that no man is "an island intire of itselfe." He meant that we do not live life as self-contained shells but as part of the total fabric of humankind. No business is an island either. Each business is woven into the total fabric of this minuscule biosphere spinning in a remote corner of an expanding universe. However, the better analogy shouldn't describe place but activity. For it is in what we do that we often find meaning in who we are, both as individuals and businesses. So let's change analogies. Let's not use an island but a butterfly instead, a butterfly described by computer-generated mathematical modeling of chaos theories.

the butterfly effect

In general, chaos theories hold that simple physical systems are inherently complex, complex systems inherently simple and that small actions at one place can create a chain of events that result in much larger, much different actions in a far-distant place. Complex computer models have described situations in which a butterfly in China can trigger air disturbances resulting in a hurricane in the Caribbean. It's called "the butterfly effect."

If butterflies can help create hurricanes, the interlocking and multiplying effects of your leadership and your business' activities also have enormous dramatic potentialities, beyond your business and even your industry. Make sure, however, that the stakes you tie your conviction to are plausible.

4. SEIZE AND FEEL THE CHANGE

Because the marketplace is constantly changing, the status quo in business is always wrong. In business, success isn't just a matter of the survival of the fittest, it is a matter of the survival of the first. You cannot be today what you were yesterday, nor can you be tomorrow what you are today. Ground your heartfelt convictions in what is changing. Everything that exists is a living seed of what will be. Casey Stengel, manager of the hapless New York Mets of the early 1960s, said to his ballclub after they lost yet another lopsided game, "You guys are getting worse every day. And today you played like tomorrow!" We show what we are by what we do with what we have, and what we have today is always a seed of tomorrow. When you let your audience see that seed, how it is an agent of change, and that you believe strongly in that change, you are well on your way to having them create — or avoid — that tomorrow.

war in the electromagnetic spectrum

It can be argued that *glasnost* and *perestroika* did not begin in 1986, when Mikhail Gorbachev first announced their establishment to the world, but in 1982. Back then, during the Israeli invasion of Lebanon, the Israeli air force shot down some 80 Syrian Migs without losing a plane and destroyed the Soviet-built armor with few tank losses on their part. A Soviet scientist saw that military technology was on a fulcrum of change. He made a speech declaring that combat technology was advancing to the point where the next world war would be fought in the electromagnetic spectrum. Mikhail Gorbachev, a young Politburo member, heard of the speech, and realized that Soviet society would have to be opened and restructured if the Soviet Union was to compete in terms of technological advancements. When Gorbachev became premier of the Soviet Union a few years later, he was motivated to begin *perestroika* and *glasnost.* Clearly, the "electromagnetic spectrum" speech was not the single, decisive factor in Mikhail Gorbachev's decision to revitalize the Soviet Union by attacking its root problems, but the speech's vision of challenge and change helped create great change in its own right.

5. FEEL YOUR BELIEF

Grant wrote Lincoln, "I was successful because you believed in me." To move people to do things, first believe that they can do those things. That belief must have feet and wings. It must be grounded in a concrete assessment of the circumstances but must challenge people to rise above the circumstances. If your audience thinks that you don't understand their reality, then they won't believe that you believe — or worse, they'll be indifferent to your belief. Do your homework. Understand their circumstances better than they do. One way is tell them something new. If they know tactics, tell them strategy. If they are immersed in order, introduce disorder. If they are rampant individualists, introduce teamwork. Whatever situation your audience is in, show them that you care by showing them that you know what they may not know. Of course, don't be smug. Always tell them what they don't know from the perspective that you are serving them.

render unto Experience

But once you've done your homework, you are only halfway home. You have rendered unto Reason but now must render unto Experience. Find something in the facts that you believe deeply in.

Don't speak unless you do! It doesn't matter what the facts are, what the situation of the audience is; you can always relate those facts and that situation to your emotions by relating them to your defining moment, which we will discuss in the next three chapters.

6. COMMUNICATE THE FEELING

Investing speeches with emotion is like hauling nitroglycerin. Handle with care. Use emotion, don't let emotion use you. Don't ring a doorbell with a howitzer shell.

When asked if he would lay down his life for his passionate convictions, Bertrand Russell said, "Of course not, I might be wrong!"

We don't trust people who show inappropriate emotion. Back in high school, I happened to play in a football game with players from across the state. Our coach was a stranger from a distant high school. Putting us through several weeks of practice before the game, he seemed normal enough. But in the locker room, just before we went out to play, he underwent a personality change. He suddenly burst into tears. "I want you to win! Win! Win!" he sobbed. His display of emotion seemed a transparent attempt to pump up our emotions. We players looked at each other as if he had grown facial hair and fangs. *Who the hell is this character?* we asked in silence. We went out onto the field not pumped up so much as a little angry at him.

communicate emotion skillfully

In my seminars on action leadership, we go through exercises to be aware of our emotions. Most seminar participants are quite good at doing that. Speaking of what moves them deeply, they often choke up and can't go on. But they are only halfway there. It's not enough for us to choke up. We must get the audience to choke up. The triumph of emotion in the motivational speech is not simply to feel it but to communicate it, to make our audience experience it.

There are two ways to communicate emotion. First, deliver it logically so they can experience it emotionally. Second, deliver it through anecdotes and stories. The following discussion will deal with the former way. The latter way will be dealt with in the next chapter.

emotion is embedded in structure

Before an audience knows what to feel, they must get the facts, understand the facts, and digest the facts. Consider evangelical sermons. Emotion is vital to them. Yet even though there are different evangelists delivering different messages on different aspects of religion, all their sermons have one thing in common: tight structure, characterized by a single idea supported by three or four subpoints.

Evangelical sermons, movies, plays, short stories, all carry emotion through structure.

Consider Hollywood movies. Nearly all of them are prefab stories, genre stories, such as comedy, love, horror, detective, action, and gangster. They are characterized by their own thematic argument, condensed philosophy and dramatic structure. Much of their emotion is embedded in and communicated from the traditional genre structure. For example, the structure of the horror story is linked to human transformation: a human becoming an animal or a machine or an animal or machine becoming human. Gangster stories have a structure based on the hero rising and falling or falling and rising and on the thematic argument of whether the means justifies the end. Love stories' genre structure are based on desire and opposition: lovers falling into and out of love or out of and into love and thereby experiencing personal growth or decline.

The point is, we can't feel until we can *logically* connect what we see with who we are. To understand this, let's conduct a psychological experiment.

crying cop

Picture a policeman, hair disheveled, coat unbuttoned, weeping uncontrollably into his hands.

We don't know what to feel about that policeman until we can understand why he is weeping.

On one hand, he might be a crazed killer who has shot at a half-dozen people, missed them all and is weeping with fury and insane disappointment.

On the other hand, he might have been standing on a bridge all night trying to talk a woman out of jumping. She has just jumped to her death, and he is heartbroken for her.

The same policeman. One image. But two different feelings we can get from that image.

Logic and structure are tracks carrying those feelings.

structuring emotion

Just as we must evaluate the ideas in a speech, so we must evaluate the emotions. One way to evaluate emotions is to view them within the context of generic structures.

1. the fable structure

A fable is a short tale with a moral. Sometimes the characters are inanimate objects or animals that teach lessons in human folly. Sometimes the characters are real enough, as in the fable I tell in Chapter 13 about one Mr. Scott, a mousetrap and a Japanese audience. Always, its moral is a call to action. In times past, fables were often highly charged political and social critiques. By making your speech or part of your speech a fable, you can make a hard-hitting point that cannot be made with objective facts. There is much folly in business, but the speaker who points it out is often derided. When you point it out through a fable and its ancient structure of fabulous-tale-teaches-moral, you enable people to step back and see that folly dispassionately and maybe even a little humorously. Make up your own fable or go to well-known fables, such as Aesop's, and retell it to suit your purposes.

2. the fairy tale structure

Fairy tales differ from fables in that the fabulous characters and events, not necessarily fairies, do not teach a moral but most often engage in family conflict that results, usually, in a happy ending. The structure is classic: a curse-fragments-family-relationships-but-is-eventually-(though not always)-overthrown. There is a metaphorical or actual journey from light into dark then back into light again. Weddings or celebrations often take place on both sides of the dark. And there is usually a helper who aids the hero when all seems lost.

This is a wonderful structure to carry your emotion. Clearly, I am not saying to communicate an overt fairy story. Instead, use the fairy story structure to carry the emotion of your message. That structure is extensively used in movies and books. *King Kong* is a fairy story. So are *A Farewell To Arms, Huckleberry Finn, The Godfather*, and *The Deer Hunter* among many examples.

A speech might be structured this way: The family could be your business; the curse, a competitive product innovation; the helper, R & D to the rescue; the celebration, a vision of new products and success. There are endless varieties of speeches that can be tied to that structure.

3. the action structure

This structure is plotted with a single strong desire line. An individual or a team has a compelling need and must overcome obstacles to fullfill that need. The emotion comes from the characters having a string of near-misses. Because action is primarily visual, the action genre was refined in movies, the classic image being the heroine tied to the railroad tracks by a villain while the hero goes through adventures to rescue her before the train arrives. The Japanese movie, *The Seven Samurai,* is one of the most powerful expressions of this genre. With this structure, you can talk about people being heroes and heroines and employ their defining moments.

physical, visual, dramatic

Make sure the action you describe takes place in crunch time, and that the action be physical, visual, and dramatic. Action movies take place every day in every business — though, clearly, they are not as visibly dramatic as people being tied to railroad tracks or swinging on vines through jungles. A person can be an action hero without moving a finger. Just sitting in one's lab creating a product innovation or at at one's desk devising a new marketing plan is action enough. As you will see in the next chapter, an executive gave a speech in which there was tremendous drama in his describing a moment in a high-school classroom when he simply raised his hand — action that changed his life.

4. the love story structure

Unlike the action genre, which takes place to a great extent in the eye, this genre takes place in the heart and involves character need. In a love story, a character has a powerful need that can only be fulfilled by one person. However, both characters clash. The love story is the clash. Love is often the opponent of both characters. Once the clash is resolved, the story is over. The clash is usually resolved by both individuals reaching beyond their self-centeredness and giving something to the other person. As in the classic love story, Shakespeare's *Romeo and Juliet*, each lover is fundamentally changed by the actions their love compells them to take.

Let's view love the way in which I explained it in the previous chapter, not as a romantic or sexual attraction, but as a manifestation of a deep need to serve a person or a cause. The love story structure, opposing-characters-find-fulfillment-and-personal-growth-through-love, is a supercharged structure that is linked to the challenges of action leadership and that can enable you to communicate powerful emotion.

5. the horror story structure

Avoid leadership by fear but do not avoid dispensing the occasional dose. Running scared is often truth in action. Sometimes we don't truly know a thing unless we fear it; although the opposite is also true: We can't know a thing *if* we fear it. To communicate that a thing should be feared, consider the classic horror-story structure. Horror-story fear is structured by loss of control. The two elements of that structure are monster and victim. The most fearful monsters, whether creatures or machines, have human aspects, and that distorted humanness is the ignition-mechanism for the fear. For the monster is truly frightening when we internalize it, when the monster threatens to become us, and we become the monster. The loss of control is, ultimately, the loss of our personal identity, or, in religious terms, the loss of our soul.

a human monster or monstrous human

The classic horror structure then is either a-monster-that-becomes-human or a-human-that-becomes-a-monster.

If you want people to fear a monster — (and in business, monsters in many guises threaten us) — then give that monster human features. Or make it human and give it a monster's features.

6. the detective story structure

Whodunit is a structured search for a solution. Using the structure loosely, you may say, "We've got a problem here, and let's come up with a solution." Or using the structure more formally, you may explain the problem and analyze a number of solutions, soliciting the audience's advice on each proposed solution. In any case, make sure the problem is stated clearly and that you and the audience agree on what the problem is before doing the detective work. The structure is an intellectual and an experiental search. Often the best detective stories don't simply search for whodunit but search also the detective's heart and soul. When you make the audience the detective too, you put their emotions into play.

several don'ts

If genres provide a structural frame to communicate emotion, then stories and anecdotes make that emotion happen. Stories have been used in speeches since time immemorial. But here are special considerations for motivating people.

— Don't moralize. Moralizing is simply another form of order leadership. On one hand, what is moral for you may not be moral for your audience, and on the other hand, you're not telling them anything new.

— Don't drag it out. People act from the emotion they get. Emotion comes quickly. Have them get it, then go on.

— Don't ridicule people. Diminishing others diminishes you and depletes the principal in the speaker/audience trust account.

ACTION TO TAKE:

— Don't bring conviction to the dance to get something from your audience. Just believe and let your audience be. Leaders do not own the people they lead. Be a leader as W.C. Fields said a gentleman should be: "A gentleman is somebody who can play the saxophone but doesn't."

— Be close to your audience not by building fences to crowd them in but by ripping up fences to let them out. Only when dancers are free to leave can they truly believe in staying.

— Know that motivational speech involves the total you, both intellectual and emotional experience. Acquiring knowledge about the audience and the speaking occasion requires that you get the facts and get the feeling. Too many leaders are masters at fact getting but not at *fact feeling*. Know that emotion is necessary, and trust your emotions and the emotions of your audience as well.

— Find the audience's emotion in the speaking occasion. It's there. It always is. In every occasion! Keep looking. You'll find it always in the audience's need. But that's not all. Gauge the intensity of the emotion by asking what is at stake in terms of the audience's need. As an exercise before speaking, lower the stakes — making the audience's need less important than they think it is. Then raise the stakes — making it more important. The stakes are flexible. Use that flexibility.

— Find the emotion in the change. Things are always changing. And like the stakes, change is flexible. Understand what the audience feels most intensely about in regard to the change.

— Once you know the audience's emotion by feeling their emotion, get to your emotion. What do you feel most strongly about in regard to the occasion and the audience's emotion? What do you absolutely believe in regard to the occasion and the audience's need? Experience that feeling before you speak.

—Use the genre structures in formal speeches and in the many informal speeches you give every day.

4

The Defining Moment

"YOU CONTROL THE present," said George Orwell, "by controlling the past." Orwell was talking about the aim of propaganda and of human enslavement. But the aim of the past/present relationship in action leadership is human liberation. Remove "control" and insert "free." We free the present by freeing the past.

That's what the defining moment is about, liberating both present and past so that people will act freely.

If action leadership enables people to arouse passion, confidence and freedom in themselves, then the techniques that best accomplish those objectives are the most powerful leadership techniques.

And one of the most powerful techniques of all is the defining moment. When you define something, you grasp its essential meaning. The defining moment, *your* defining moment, is simply a moment in your past, your most naked and wonderful moment, which helped define who you are now.

THE GREAT QUESTION

A great question hangs in the air every time one person speaks and the other listens — whether or not the speaker or the listener are conscious of that question. It's simply, WHY AM I HERE?

Both people in the motivational dance are brought together in a moment rich in existential importance.

An ancient Chinese poem says,

In an eternity of endless space,
A day of winds and moon.

This moment that we meet is grounded in time and space, in our immediate needs and situation, in "a day of winds and moon," but the moment is also integrated with "an eternity of endless space." Our births, our childhood, our education, our choices, our mistakes and successes, our joys and sorrows, our loving and hating, our living and dreaming and striving, all come together in the moment of the dance. Not only that but all the influences of an endless universe in eternity come together as well. (For instance, only hydrogen and helium composed the early universe. All other elements were formed by exploding stars. Our bodies are composed of the byproducts of ancient supernovas.) Those influences converge not in any abstract philosophical sense but in a practical sense in which all of the past *is* the present. That is a business lesson!

DIFFERENT WAYS OF KNOWING

To dance, both the speaker and the audience must know each other. But we need to know each other in different ways.

We come to know our audience by understanding their needs. In most cases, the audience couldn't care less about our needs. They are only concerned about their needs. Audiences couldn't care less about our good intentions. ("Good intentions," said a client of mine, "have a half-life of a week and are soluble in alcohol.") Still, the audience needs to know who we are. But they want to know *why am I, the speaker, here?* Who we are, in terms of the audience's need to know, is why we are here. The defining moment answers that question.

WHY THE DEFINING MOMENT?

Clearly, each one of us has had many defining experiences in our life. Furthermore, since life is a continuum of experiences, those experiences that have shaped us often occur over months and years.

But for the purposes of motivating people, of answering WHY AM I HERE?, of dancing, we must use a defining moment, not a defining experience. A defining moment is a defining experience minus time. It is that single moment in our past that brought us to this present.

Each individual life is a tracer shot into the long night of the universe — but that tracer is everything.

So those defining moments of our lives — those moments when we were changed forever — are tracers of experience that mean everything to action leadership.

DEFINING MOMENTS IN HISTORY

"This night," wrote Albert Camus in his journal during the liberation of Paris in 1945, "is worth a world." Moments do count. They are defining. And they can be worth a world.

When Archimedes in ancient Syracuse lowered himself into a tub, saw water spill over the sides, understood immediately that the weight and volume of his body caused the displacement of water, and went running naked through the streets crying, "Eureka! I've found the answer!" — that was a defining moment in the history of science.

When in 1589, a 25-year-old mathematics instructor at the University of Pisa in Italy, Galileo Galilei, dropped two cannonballs from the Leaning Tower of Pisa, one weighing 10 pounds and the other 1 pound, and both cannonballs hit the ground at the same time, thus destroying a 2,000-year-old assertion of Aristotle that heavy objects fall faster than light objects — that was a defining moment of the Renaissance.

When in 1928 in London, England the Scottish biologist Alexander Fleming, studying bacteria that caused boils, happened to notice that mold contaminated cultures in several of his petri dishes, he observed that no bacteria grew around the edges of the mold — that moment of observation was a defining moment in medicine, from which flowed the discovery of penicillin and other antibiotics.

When in 1917, a mob of St. Petersburg citizens, armed only with clubs, was storming the czar's Winter Palace and a guard at the front gate, instead of firing on the crowd, stood aside and winked, in that wink was a defining moment that led to the Bolshevik takeover, the fall of the Russian empire and the rise of the Soviet empire.

YOUR DEFINING MOMENT

You too have had your defining moments. You need at most two or three to prepare a lifetime of motivational speeches. But before we get into how to use the defining moment, let's understand why it is important.

1. IT REVEALS YOUR PERSONAL SELF

Pittsburgh Pirate home run hitter of the 1950s, Ralph Kiner, was asked why he didn't choke up on the bat and swing easier to get more hits and reduce his strike-outs. "Cadillacs," he said, "are down at the end of my bat."

As an action leader, you must see yourself as a let-'er-rip home run hitter. Be willing to swing from the heels by taking emotional risks. Be willing to reveal your heartfelt emotions and experiences. Heartfelt speech leads to heartfelt action.

In a seminar, a president of a company said, "Brent, I can't bring my personal self into my business life. I'm one person from nine to five. I'm another person at other times. I'm not going to mix them up."

the bifurcated leader

My response: Only order leaders have the luxury of bifurcating themselves. They don't have to make a vital human connection with the people to whom they give orders. Order leadership is about human separation. Action leadership is about human integration. By standing apart from people, order leaders often stand apart from themselves, dividing into business and personal halves. Because action leaders get close to people emotionally, they bring the totality of their selves into the dance. They must take risks by revealing their personal selves.

personal vs. private

Let's make a distinction between personal and private in regard to the defining moment. Action leadership is not about communicating the private you. It's about communicating the *personal* you. The difference between private and personal is embarrassment. In checking out your defining moment, embarrassment is a sign that you are on the wrong track. It's been said that you can't write a good autobiography unless you're writing about what embarrasses you. But in action leadership, if you feel embarrassed by what you reveal, you have crossed the line from personal to private. Don't use it. If you're uncomfortably self-conscious, your audience will most likely be too. And when they are uncomfortable with what you said, you are not communicating a defining moment. In one seminar, an executive told of his being beaten as a child by his grandfather, sometimes to the point of unconsciousness. His revelation was shocking, and it caused us to feel sorry for him. But it didn't relate to motivating people to take action. He couldn't tie it to the needs of the audience or the emotion of the situation. There was no redemption to it. It wasn't a defining personal moment. It was a defining *private* moment, and defining private moments should never be used.

2. IT CONDENSES AND CONTROLS THE EMOTION

The defining moment enables you to condense and control the emotion in your speech and gives your personal revelation structure, direction and depth. Self revelation is still risky, but it is risk taken by the skilled artist rather than the rank beginner.

In one of my seminars, a CEO related an incident in which he killed a man in hand-to-hand combat in Germany. "It was a defining moment in my life," he said. "In that moment, I went from being a fresh-faced boy who just arrived on the front lines to being an old man. It changed the whole way I see and live life."

It was a moment that led to his becoming a lifelong pacifist, pacifism that characterized much of his business style and philosophy. When he began compressing, developing and communicating his defining moment to audiences, revealing the personal aspects of his business dealings, he began to transform himself from an inveterate order leader to an action leader.

raising a hand

But not all defining moments are so overtly dramatic as hand-to-hand combat. Often, their powerful impact comes from a look or a simple gesture.

The following is a section of a speech given by a top executive of a publishing firm before his sales audience.

The audience was in a tough sales market. He had just taken on his job and had to communicate the fact that he was deeply committed to their success.

He said,

"We touch the future with our children's hands."

I'm sure that you have heard that saying before.

It reflects why I'm convinced that every one of us in this room is in the best profession . . . and yes, best business . . . in the world.

And why you're going to win this big sales battle.

Yet that saying points to a deeper truth. A truth that doesn't simply describe why we are here . . . but more importantly, what we must do . . . the experience we must share and put into action after we leave here.

But for you to understand that deeper truth . . . I want to share an experience with you.

Yes, we do touch the future with our children's hands. And some years ago, a boy sitting in a homeroom class in Nebraska saw his future. He saw it so clearly, so vividly that he could just about touch it.

It was springtime of his senior year, and the homeroom teacher asked his class, "Who is going to attend the University of Nebraska next year?"

The boy looked around him. Many of his classmates had their hands raised.

It was a revelation to the boy. He hadn't really given much thought to what he would do after high school.

Then he did something that changed his life forever.

He raised his hand too.

He decided right then and there that he too was going on to college, and his hand was up!

Sounds like a story with a happy ending. The boy goes on and is a great success.

The trouble was it didn't have a happy ending. The boy didn't succeed. He failed miserably.

You see, the boy couldn't read very well. He had taken vocational courses throughout his high school years. Not precollege courses.

He was totally unprepared for the heavy reading load at the University.

He studied hard, but it was no use. He flunked out at the end of the first semester.

Bitter and angry, he joined the Army and ended up shoveling coal and cleaning artillery pieces for four years in Germany.

That's the experience I wanted to share . . . the experience that points to a deeper truth about why we are here and the action we have to take.

You see, the boy was me. I was the one sitting in the homeroom class. I was the one who raised my hand. I was the one who wanted to have an educated life so bad that I could taste it. I was the one who flunked out and spent the next four years in the Army.

Here's the point.

Certainly, we touch the future with our children's hands — but in a deeper sense, we make the future happen through our children's minds.

Through the transformation of our children's minds to day, we actually transform the future, long before it ever happens.

That is our opportunity in this sales battle.

We are making the future take place, long before it ever happens.

I'm here today, speaking to you, for this very simple reason. Three decades ago, when I raised my hand in that homeroom class, I knew down deep that I couldn't cut it. It was one of the worst feelings I think I've ever had. Because suddenly I realized I didn't have any choices, because I knew that I wasn't prepared. I'm here because my career has been a kind of vow to do the best I can not to have other children have that feeling . . .to bring choices, and a future, to children . . . no matter what their color, no matter what their culture, no matter what their income status.

That's why you're in this room too. You don't have a job, you have a vow. It's my vow. But more important, it should be your vow.

Yes, we have big challenges ahead of us.

Yes, we have terrific competition to overcome.

But we're going to meet those challenges . . .
we're going to overcome that competition . . . as long as we understand this very simple truth: that our products, our programs, our strategies . . . all come from one place, our hearts

. . . . that our sales strategy is first and foremost a feeling . . . a commitment . . . a passion.

A feeling . . . a commitment . . . a passion that you must experience yourself to share it with others.

prototype motivational speech

Here was a prototypical motivational speech. That moment decades ago when he raised his hand — and revealed himself to his audience today — was worth a world.

3. IT COMMUNICATES EMOTION

If the defining moment did not have powerful emotion, it would not be a defining moment. Its emotion lends a kind of poetry to your words, and the poetry of your words helps communicate that emotion. But if there were a direct correlation between the powerful emotion you display and the feelings your audience gets, then the best motivational speeches would indeed be linked to your ability to foam at the mouth. Being a kind of poem, a motivational speech communicates emotion not through your emoting but through your applying many of the techniques of poetry, such as metaphor, simile and image. English poet William Wordsworth said that poetry is "powerful emotion recollected in tranquility."

active tranquility

Take Wordsworth's advice: Cultivating tranquility is the secret of communicating emotion. However, it is the tranquility of inactivity and also activity. Be actively tranquil. That means find tranquility in working hard and well. Communicating emotion *is* work, with inspiration the numerator and perspiration the denominator. German playwright and poet Bertolt Brecht said that during the intermissions of his plays he wanted the curtain to be lowered only halfway so that the audience could see stagehands moving scenery and know that good theater entailed hard work.

We'll examine how to develop and communicate the defining moment in subsequent chapters. The point is that when properly developed, it's the Swiss Army knife of communicating emotion: practical, adaptable and enduring.

4. IT REVEALS THE AUDIENCE TO THEMSELVES

Your defining moment doesn't exist for you. It exists for your audience. You remember it, develop it, and communicate it so that your audience can take action that will make them better than they are. The defining moment is useless if it does not help the audience fulfill their need.

So in relating your defining moment, be aware of the switch-point, that point in your talk in which you tell the audience in unmistakable terms not *look what I did!* but *look what you can do!*

Thus the publishing executive says, "The experience I share with you points to a deeper truth about why we are here and the action we must take."

5. IT GIVES ADDED COMMITMENT TO THE ACTION

"How respectable is earnestness on every platform," said Ralph Waldo Emerson, "but intellect kills it." Next to what we do, the most concrete facts of life aren't what we think but what we feel. William Butler Yeats said, "We taste and feel and see the truth. We do not reason ourselves into it." The defining moment gives taste and feel to the truth on which action is based. When our executive talked about raising his hand in the homeroom class, the power of his experience gave deeper meaning to the action he challenged them to take. If he communicated his defining moment effectively, they were back there with him in the classroom, rooting for him as he raised his hand. Furthermore, in a deeper sense, they raised their hands too, not just then but now when he tied the moment to his call to action.

6. IT RAISES THE STAKES

The action you want your audience to take need not be extraordinary. In fact, that action is often most effective when it is ordinary. Sometimes just having your audience pick up a phone and dial a number is enough. But that does not mean your speech is mundane. Small action should always take place against a large backdrop. Keep the stakes high. Keep the future exciting.

Former heavyweight champ Archie Moore said, "I knew *how* to fight early. I learned that. More important is to learn what to fight for. I was fighting for my family, for my future; I was fighting for, generally, the black race, for men who had given up their lives. You got to know *what* you're fighting for. Then the fight is much easier."

When your defining moment is exciting because it involves what you are fighting for, when it points to the higher stakes you want your audience to buy into, then the action they take is more important to them. Our executive raised the stakes for his audience by saying that he didn't have a job but a vow — and in doing so raised the stakes for his sales force and made their future, and their prospects, more exciting.

7. IT HUMBLES

King Canute of England, who lived 1,000 years ago, was either the dumbest or the wisest of men. His subjects constantly showered him with flattery. One day he had his throne brought to the seashore. Sitting down, he commanded the waves to stop. Of course, the tide rolled in and soaked him. He gave up his kingship and became a beggar.

On one hand, anybody who thinks he can command waves to stop is probably a quart low. On the other hand, there might have been madness in Canute's method — the divine madness of an enlightened sage. For seen in a different way, Canute's actions were an expostulation on power and leadership. Since waves can't be commanded to stop, then the trappings of kings are the toys of fools. Better to be a beggar, Canute might have been saying, than a fool of a king.

of the soil

The King Canute lesson might be seen as one of humility and leadership. The motivational dance is humility in action. If you come across as having a blimp-sized ego, you'll bump against and irritate rather than motivate people. A big ego is a big problem for a motivational leader — though often the order leader thrives on it. But don't cultivate being a doormat. A weak, submissive, indecisive person motivates others poorly. There is a momentous difference in having a strong ego, or strong knowledge that, as a preacher said, "you are a child of the universe, no less than the trees and stars, and that you have a right to be here," and having a big ego, inward-focused and endothermic.

Strong leadership is a manifestation of strong ego. Be humble, not in a demeaning, self-pitying sense but in an affirming, joyful sense. Humility is soil for the roots of action leadership. In fact, the word *humility* derives from *humus,* soil. So does the word *human.* To be truly human is to possess humility, to be of the soil. Philip of Macedonia gave two soldiers what many considered the most ludicrous of jobs but which Philip thought the most important. In the morning, one soldier said, to him, "You are nothing but a man." In the evening, the other soldier said, "You are nothing but a man." We never rise higher than when we return to the soil. "Humility, like darkness," said Thoreau, "reveals the heavenly lights."

achievement and change

Don't talk about what you achieved in your moment but what changed you. Don't talk about your being covered with glory but of being uncovered in the soil of human tragedy and comedy. In our executive's speech, it was only toward the end that he said he taught himself to read while in the Army and went back to get degrees from Nebraska and Harvard. But that revelation came only as an epilogue. If the audience had thought it was the message, he wouldn't have communicated a defining moment but instead have simply engaged in an exercise in chest-thumping.

8. IT AVOIDS CLICHES

You are asked to motivate an employee to run a 100-meter dash against your competition. The winner wins the customer. As your runner approaches the starting line, you help her on with your specially made gear: diver's lead boots. You cheer enthusiastically as the gun sounds and she tries to get out of the blocks.

spurring donkeys

Motivating people with cliches is as helpful as diver's boots to the runner. Cliches are overused expressions that at best do little for motivation and at worst drop it with a brain-shot in its tracks. If you're ready to undertake a difficult task, and your boss tries to psych you up by saying, "Don't forget, when the going gets tough, the tough get going!", or "When you spur a race horse it runs, when you spur a donkey, it kicks!" or "Do your best and you'll be the best!", you'll probably get a severe case of the "Yeah . . . sure!" syndrome.

unique you

By using your defining moment — measuring it against the check list in the next chapter — you are guaranteed not to be speaking cliches. For the defining moment comes not from the re-fried hash of the overly used but from the freshly picked of your unique experiences. There never was any one like you since the beginning of the universe. There never will be any one like you again. Each defining moment of yours scintillates and motivates. In every seminar I've conducted in which people relate their defining moments, I have been moved by powerful, original images, images that move me still.

ACTION TO TAKE:

Use your defining moment to motivate your audience *and* yourself. Before preparing a speech, go back to your moment, ask:

— Why is it important in relationship to the dramatic situation in which I speak?

— Why is it important to the audience's need?

— Why is it important to the action I want them to take?

5

Characteristics of the Defining Moment

"YOU CAN PUT on the most glamorous, high-rated show in the world," said Will Rogers, "but it's no good if you can't find a way to sell soap on it."

The defining moment is not style but substance. If it doesn't "sell soap," if it doesn't enhance your value as a leader, if it doesn't work in the marketplace, then it's academic flapdoodle.

But the promise of this book is that the defining moment does sell soap. Through it, your audience will not only hear but experience what you say — and by experiencing what you say, take the action you want them to take. Before we get into how to find and use the defining moment, let's understand what soap-selling features it must have.

1. THE DEFINING MOMENT MUST BE DRAMATIC

"When in doubt," Raymond Chandler advised writers, "have

two guys come through the door with guns." A key objective of leadership is to make things exciting.

So make your defining moment exciting. Clearly, if that moment you experienced changed you forever, it must be dramatic. The more dramatic it is, the more powerfully it can motivate others.

2. IT MUST BE A MOMENT ONLY

Make sure that the experience takes place in a moment and not a month or year. Doing so gives unity and a dramatic framework to the experience, and freeze-frames it in the audience's mind. That emotion-charged freeze-frame is a motivation trigger.

3. IT MUST HAVE CHANGED YOU PROFOUNDLY

"Get used to thinking," wrote Marcus Aurelius, "that there is nothing nature loves more than to change existing forms. The universe is change. Our life is what our thoughts make of it."

You entered the moment as one person, were changed, then moved away from the moment fundamentally changed.

An executive told me about his squad getting ambushed in Vietnam. He alone survived the ambush. Hiding in grass, he watched the small Viet Cong unit file off into the jungle. One by one the Viet Cong soldiers filed past without seeing him. But the last one turned and looked right at him. For a terrible moment, they stared at each other. "All he had to do was pull the trigger and I was dead," he said. "But then he did something that astonished me. He turned away and kept walking. He gave me my life. Because of that moment, all the years since, every day I give as much as I can to people."

4. IT MUST BE TIED TO THE AUDIENCE'S NEED

Because the speaker exists for the audience and not the audience for the speaker, it must be clear to your audience that your defining moment lives in the present to help fulfill their need. If you don't connect your defining moment with your audience's need, then that moment is merely an act of self-indulgence.

In the last chapter, we saw that the sales force's clear need was to have confidence in their boss's leadership. So he shared his defining moment with them so that they could understand why he was so committed to supporting them.

5. IT MUST BE TIED TO YOUR PASSIONATE CONVICTION

A successful magazine writer once told me, "A good writer can make anything interesting. If you're worth your salt, you could turn out a fascinating piece on a doorknob. And you do that by being able to write well and *then having a deep conviction about that doorknob.*"

Conviction can raise leadership speech from doldrums to drumbeat. You cannot get people to act if you don't believe deeply in those people, what you say to them and the action you want them to take. You must, if you're worth your salt as a leader, find conviction in every speaking situation.

"Just close your fingers."

One of my defining moments happened when my father was dying of cancer a few years ago. We had become very close during those years after his diagnosis, the illness giving us an opportunity to heal our relationship, which had once been strained. A few weeks before his death, I was talking to him as he lay in his bed. As he and I talked about a great many things, his mind sharp as always, he having to take only low doses of pain-killing drugs, I told him that I seemed to have run out of opportunities in my life. I had been trying to start a new business and seemed to have stuffed myself in a career drawer, with no way out. He said, "Brent, you have opportunities. Everybody has opportunities. They're in your hand. Just close your fingers." Then this man, wracked with cancer, near death, his skin hanging transparently on his skeleton frame, actually laughed, laughed in a quiet, kindly way and said what I'll never forget, "Look at me, Brent, even *I* have opportunities. Even if it is only the opportunity to love you."

And now when I give lectures and seminars and talk about business opportunities, I bring that moment back in my heart and often in my words and speak about how we all have opportunities. If my father on his deathbed could say with deep conviction, "Even I have opportunities," then we just have to reach out and close our fingers.

6. IT MUST BE TIED TO ACTION

At the end of his speech to his sales force in the last chapter, the leader applied a fundamental motivational technique: He challenged them to challenge him.

> *Because of my experience in that classroom in Nebraska more than three decades ago, I don't have a job. I have a vow. A vow to make students better readers and thus transform their future and ours.*

He told the sales people to write him a letter the next day that would challenge him in three specific ways to help them better increase their sales.

He concluded:

Whatever day. Whatever hour. Where ever you are. If you need me, I'll be there for you. Together we're going to transform the future.

7. IT MUST BE VISUAL

Seeing is believing. But believing is also seeing. For people to feel things, they must see them so they can believe them. Think of the defining moment as a scene in a movie. See in your mind's eye a boy raising his hand in a homeroom classroom. See a Viet Cong soldier turn and look into the bush. Every defining moment must be visualized. It's not enough that you communicate the emotion you got; you must describe the visual facts that gave you that emotion. Then your audience will get the emotion on their own account, without your having to tell them what to feel.

8. IT MUST HAVE CHARACTER

The defining moment isn't a still-life. It is character in action. And what is character in terms of the defining moment? *Character is need in action.* The moment he raised his hand, knowing that he couldn't read well, but committing himself nonetheless to going to the university, we immediately understood his character. Then and now.

9. IT MUST BE BRIEF

The one ingredient that too many leaders' speeches have is boredom. Some leaders have raised boredom to an almost mystical experience and so have become some of the mystical gurus of our time. In many cases, you have to speak up to be noticed and shut up to be interesting. Keep your defining moment brief. An audience member after one long speech said, "He not only wastes time — he encroaches on eternity." A great salesman told me that he makes a point of being the first person to rise and begin to conclude any sales situation. Helen Hayes' advice to performers, "Always leave them wanting more," applies to the defining moment as well. Another piece of advice, this from an actor friend of mine: "Get on the stage. Plant your feet. Say your lines. Then get right off." Ditto for the defining moment. Get it right. State it right. (Be able to summarize it in an absolutely understandable way in one sentence.) Then get on with the rest of your speech.

10. IT MUST BE REPEATABLE.

In my seminars, the question often comes up: How can I use only several defining moments for a lifetime of speeches? Aren't people going to get sick of hearing about it?

Yes, they are if you keep repeating it the same way. Looked at in a shallow way, the defining moment is a one-shot technique. But seen in the context of action leadership, it is an emotional mother lode that becomes ever more abundant the more it is used.

make it count by leaving it out

Your defining moment should be in every motivational speech you give, but it does not have to be explicitly stated. As a leader, you speak many times to the same audience. Clearly, if you already communicated your defining moment to that audience, you don't have to tell it to them, word for word, all over again. In fact, the defining moment often is most powerful not when you put it in, but when you leave it out, when they already know all about it as you speak.

A recent figure-skating champion was born with two club feet. One reason she did so well under pressure was that the real pressure

— the operations she endured — was over by the time she came out on the ice. She won the gold, and her defining experience of undergoing painful operations was implicit in and gave poignant beauty to her skating.

enriched with use

Opera lovers testify that the human voice is enriched and made increasingly resonant as an opera unfolds. When given proper training, vocal cords become a more effective singing instrument through demanding use. Often, at the end of the opera, a voice sounds much richer and purer than at its beginning. So with the defining moment . . . . It's not a perishable commodity. Like the human voice, it too is enriched through use.

There are many ways to use it: The sales leader told it in the third person, then said that he was talking about himself; you can tell it from the standpoint of other characters who were involved in it (e.g., from the homeroom teacher's standpoint); ask the audience to picture themselves going through the experience; tell it in the present tense; break it up and tell it in tantalizing fragments throughout the speech; put the audience in the place of the main character. (For instance, our executive could have said: "Picture yourself, sitting in a homeroom classroom and the teacher asks who is going to the university. You look around. Your friends are raising their hands. You know you can't read well enough to go yourself but you raise your hand anyway. What do you feel at that moment? Can anyone tell me?")

11. IT MUST BE OPTIMISTIC

If it wasn't for the optimist, the pessimist wouldn't know how happy he isn't. Unhappiness is a poor attribute of leadership. Action is the function of every motivational speech. The call to action is a leap of faith, a challenge of optimism. You cannot challenge somebody to tackle difficulties you yourself think are insurmountable. You must, as the Johnny Mercer song advises, "Accentuate the positive. Eliminate the negative."

There is no loss in business, there is only change. The difference between failure and success is often how we see a situation and what we make of it. Order leaders might see the tunnel in every light and continue to function quite well. But action leaders must see the light in every tunnel. They know that great opportunities often come gift-wrapped as unsolvable problems. When one door closes in our face, another door opens somewhere else. Often we are so distraught by the closed door that we fail to see the open door.

Good leaders are constantly seeking — so they can constantly find. The quintessential action leader was Shakespeare's Henry V. Sometimes he's been viewed as a war-mongering loudmouth. But a close examination of the play reveals that Henry is a 15th-century king with 1990s action-leadership characteristics, a leader who doesn't simply give orders but dances, who always sees an open door.

Agincourt

Just before the Battle of Agincourt on that clear October day in 1415, when his army, weary from long marches and hard battles and depleted by dysentery, faced a rested and better-equipped French force, five times its size, formed on high ground, Henry's officers believed that there was no light in the tunnel, that all the doors to victory were closed.

Henry's cousin, Westmoreland, remarks, "O that we now had here but one ten thousand of those men in England that do no work today!"

But Henry sees the light in the tunnel and reproves

Westmoreland:

"God's will! I pray thee, wish not one man more.
By Jove, I am not covetous for gold,
Nor care I who doth feed upon my cost;
It yearns me not if men my garments wear;
Such outward things dwell not in my desires;
But if it be a sin to covet honour
I am the most offending soul alive.
No, faith, my coz, wish not a man from England.
God's peace! I would not lose so great an honour
As one man more, methinks, would share from me
For the best hope I have. O, do not wish one more!
Rather proclaim it, Westmoreland, through my host,
That which hath no stomach to this fight,
Let him depart; his passport shall be made,
And crowns for convoy put into his purse:
We would not die in that man's company
That fears his fellowship to die with us.
This day is call'd the feast of Crispian:
He that outlives this day, and comes safe home,
Will stand a tip-toe when this day is nam'd,
And rouse him at the name of Crispian.
He that shall live this day, and see old age,
Will yearly on the vigil feast his neighbours,
And say, "Tomorrow is Saint Crispian."
Then he will strip his sleeve and show his scars
And say, "These wounds I had on Crispian's day."
Old men forget; yet all shall be forgot,
But he'll remember with advantages
What feats he did that day. Then shall our names,
Familiar in his mouth as household words,
Harry the king, Bedford, and Exeter,
Warwick and Talbot, Salisbury and Gloucester,

Be in their flowing cups freshly remember'd.
This story shall the good man teach his son;
And Crispin Crispian shall ne'er go by.
From this day to the ending of the world,
But we in it shall be remember'd,
We few, we happy few, we band of brothers;
For he today that shed his blood with me
Shall be my brother; be he ne'er so vile,
This day shall gentle his condition;
And gentlemen in England now a-bed
Shall think themselves accurs'd they were not here,
And hold their manhoods cheap whiles any speaks
That fought with us upon Saint Crispin's day.

Analyze this speech. It provides a template for action leadership. Henry doesn't covet riches. He's raised the stakes to more sublime levels. He covets honor. Certainly, in his love of honor, there is the hint of a defining moment here. He's not ordering his soldiers to fight. Just the opposite. He tells them that if they do not want to fight, he will give them money and safe passage home. He makes it *their* choice. He gives them freedom — and, paradoxically, binds them all the more closely to him and his cause. Through the force of his personality, through his words (Napoleon's biographer said that in the Italian campaign, half of Napoleon's success was attributable to his words), Henry transformed a breakdown into a breakthrough, made a sow's ear into a silk purse, convincing even pessimistic Westmoreland. For when Henry, after his speech asked, "*Thou dost not wish more help from England, coz?*" Westmoreland replied,

God's will! my liege, would you and I alone,
Without more help, could fight this royal battle!

wrong interpretation

Sir Laurence Olivier and many other actors and directors interpret the speech as a kind of rousing, shouting pep talk, as if people are motivated by bombast and blarney — when in fact that speech could very well, should very well, be spoken calmly and deliberately. If you want people to listen, if you want to rouse them to do great deeds, don't shout, speak low.

Like Henry at Agincourt, an action leader must be able to see the good news in every bad-news situation and transform that bad into good. So every defining moment must be ultimately uplifting.

the optimism trap

I use the "light at the end of the tunnel" cliche to point out that unbridled optimism can be a fatal trap. A latter-day Westmoreland, Gen. William Westmoreland, fell victim to the optimism trap by giving the American public optimistic reports of the progress of United States and South Vietnamese troops during the mid-1960s. In September 1966, President Lyndon B. Johnson said, "I believe there is a light at what has been a long and lonely tunnel" — unknowingly echoing French General Henri-Eugene Navarre who said 13 years before, just before the battle of Dien Ben Phu, "Now we can see (victory) clearly — like light at the end of a tunnel."

blindness of the heart

"In war, false ideas proceeding from the blindness of the heart," said German military analyst Karl von Clausewitz, "are the worst ideas." The optimism of a leader must be based not on wishful thinking but on sound judgment. Keep that "light at the end of the tunnel" phrase in mind — in regard to both its best and worst meanings. Always watch for the light — knowing that it might be instead a search team looking for survivors. The art of action leadership is understanding the difference before anybody else does.

6

Developing the Defining Moment

Recently, I was invited to lecture on leadership communication to members of an executive MBA class at a large university. Due to a printing error in the confirmation letter, I thought I was expected to speak for an hour and a half. But when I arrived, I discovered that the audience expected me to speak for five straight hours. I gazed at the students, most of whom were midlevel managers, and remembered advice given by former middleweight champ, Beau Jack: "If you're not in great condition when you go into that ring, you're gonna get your brains splattered to the other side of your head." Wondering what the hell I was going to say for five hours, without getting TKOed, i.e., having large segments of the audience nod off on me or walk out, I experienced a minor defining moment. I began by asking a question.

YELTSIN ON THE TANK/DUKAKIS IN A TANK

The image of Boris Yeltsin standing atop the tank in August 1991 came to mind. I asked, "What's the difference between Boris Yeltsin standing on a tank and Michael Dukakis in the 1988 presidential campaign riding in a tank?"

One could provide many answers dealing with leadership communication, but I wasn't concerned with answers so much as I was using the question to probe the audience and myself. Listening to their answers, I was reminded of Socrates teaching by questioning. The Delphic oracle said that Socrates was the wisest of Athenians. Socrates said he was wise because he knew nothing. Knowing nothing, he had nothing to teach. If Socrates had nothing to teach, who had the answers? The students, of course. If these students already have the answers inside them, then my teaching does not involve simply pouring information into their heads. If I did that, I could not have spoken more than 50 minutes. My teaching didn't involve my giving them anything. They had what they needed. My teaching involved simply helping them become aware of what they already have. The rest was my supplying techniques.

YOU HAVE THE ANSWERS

By concentrating on helping the students discover what they already possessed, the five hours was up in a flash. We had an exciting and informative time coming to understand the embarrassment of riches they possess in regard to their becoming action leaders.

So it is with your defining moment. You have the answers, I don't. I might be able to show you a path to your defining moment. But you have to go up the path yourself. In fact, there are many paths to it. The one I show you in this chapter is not necessarily the best one for you. It is merely a jumping-off point for your journey. Here is a three-step overview on developing your defining moment: Review, recall, refine.

1. REVIEW

The first step in developing the defining moment is to review the present speaking situation. Don't ask, what happened in my past? Ask: *What is happening now*? In terms of the defining moment in action leadership, *the past must be now.*

Clearly, everybody has many, powerful defining moments to draw on. That is not the challenge. The challenge is to pick the right one, and, by developing and communicating it properly, make right action happen. After all, you don't want the audience to think of you the way Samuel Johnson thought of a speaker in his time, "That fellow possesses but one idea and that is the wrong one."

answer needs

To get an indication of what is happening now, reread Chapter 2 and answer *What does the audience need?* However, understanding audience needs doesn't provide the whole story. After all, an audience might misunderstand what is happening now. For instance, they might not understand the full extent of difficulties they must encounter to achieve a goal. Or they might want to rest when you want them to run, or run when you want them to rest.

So you must answer two more questions to understand what is happening now.

what does the situation need?

Every speaking situation that calls for people to take action has a dramatic flashpoint. Understand and communicate that flashpoint. You can understand it by asking, *what does the situation need?*

Ancient Athenian statesman and orator Demosthenes once tried to address a public assembly of Athenians about curtailing the power of Macedonia. But the audience shouted angrily at him, refusing to listen. Demosthenes then told a story of a man who hired an ass to take him home in the summer. "In the hot afternoon, the man and the ass's owner decided to stop and rest," Demosthenes said. "The man sat down in the shadow of the ass. But the owner of the ass pushed him away. 'I own the ass, so I own its shadow,' the owner said. The man replied, 'I hired the ass, so I hired its shadow.'" Then Demosthenes stopped speaking and started to walk away. But the crowd shouted for him to stay. Intent on how the story would come out, they insisted that he keep talking. Demosthenes said, "Look at you, you want to know about the shadow of an ass but not about the danger Macedonia poses to your liberties!" Taken aback by this truth, the crowd let Demosthenes speak. So powerful was Demosthenes' speech that the audience forgot about the ass and its shadow. To this day, we don't know who won the quarrel over the shadow of the ass.

Demonsthenes understood and communicated the need of that situation.

what does the speaker need?

In the previous chapter, I talked about your focusing first on the audience's needs, not yours. But don't neglect your own needs. Be clear about what you need in the speaking situation. Keep in touch with reality, i.e., see what you see — not what you want to see or what other people want you to see or what you are conditioned *not* to see. "The true mystery of this world," said Oscar Wilde, "is the visible, not the invisible." The threat of Macedonian military power was not yet visible to the Athenians, but it was tangible to Demosthenes. Demosthenes needed to make that threat tangible to the Athenians. If he had rebuked them or argued with them, he might have satisfied his anger and made that anger tangible to the crowd but not his need. Instead, he understood clearly what he needed: to make them see what they were conditioned not to see, that upstart Macedonia truly threatened great Athens.

the art of the answers

The answers to the three questions — What does the audience need? What does the situation need? What does the speaker need? — help you know what is happening now. The questions are my techniques, the knowledge yours. You may give priority to your audience's need or the situation's need or you may combine needs. How you select, synthesize or scrap the answers is the art of determining what is happening now. It cannot be taught but is ultimately shaped through trial and error and constant regulation in your experience. Ask the three questions at every speaking situation. If you are to be an effective action leader, knowing what is happening now must go on always.

2. RECALL

Once you know what is happening now, you are ready to begin recalling your defining moment.

The first step involves belief. Believe in yourself, not just your "I think therefore I am" individual self — but your unconscious, universal Self. Know that your past encompasses your own remembrances and also humanity's past, in fact the past of the universe.

You might ask, *what does all that have to do with my fourth-quarter numbers?*

It doesn't, if you're an order leader.

It does, if you dance.

To dance as an action leader, keep your spirit lithe and young. Take Bill "Bojangles" Robinson's advice: "I won't be old till my feet hurt. And they only hurt when I don't let them dance enough. So I'll keep right on dancing!" As Bojangles used his feet, you must use your past. Exploring and using the abundance of your past will enable you to keep right on dancing.

Indra's net

That all things in the universe are interconnected, that each one of us are flowers in a flowering cosmos, is not a new idea. Throughout history, mystics of most religions have testified in one way or the other to that truth. Some 1,500 years ago, a deeply enlightened Chinese sage, Hua-yen, spoke of the universe as being like Indra's net, a net of pearls covering the goddess Indra's palace. Each pearl reflects all the other pearls. Take one pearl in your hand and you take them all. See into one and you see into them all. Each thing in the universe, Hua-yen said, each grain of sand, each individual person, each blade of grass, each animal, each cell, is a pearl in Indra's net, unique in its individuality yet reflecting the whole.

Bell's theorem

This metaphor is borne out in science and technology. Beginning with the formulation of Bell's theorem in 1964, scientists proved that two subatomic particles, two pearls in Indra's net, once having interacted with each other in terms of the axis of their spin, remain in sync (always spinning in opposite directions) no matter how far apart they are. The axis of spin can be chosen by the way in which the observer measures it. Let's say the spin is clockwise, then the companion particle will be spinning counterclockwise. If the spin is counterclockwise, the companion particle will be spinning clockwise. *It doesn't matter if the particles are one mile or 1 billion miles apart!* Somehow the particles are communicating instantly. But according to the laws of relativity, that communication is impossible, since the fastest communication between two points is the speed of light. So maybe they aren't communicating! Maybe they are able to stay in sync because *in reality, there is no distance between them.* The space between them may simply be a temporary manifestation of a single as-yet-unknown reality.

the universe as a holograph

We can touch and see this interconnectedness in a holograph. A holograph is made by imprinting a wave front of what is called coherent light (light whose waves are in step with each other) onto a photographic plate to make a three-dimensional image. A cylindrical holograph can be made that reveals the outer surfaces of an image. A person can walk around the cylinder and see the image's front and back. Turn the cylinder upside down and new views of the image appear. But that's not all. Any section of the holograph can be used to re-create the whole image. That's because the holograph repeats the same wave front many times across its entire surface. Think of the universe as a holograph, vastly richer, more dynamic, containing many more dimensions than a photographic holograph, and you have Indra's net once again.

the leader as a holograph

If the order leader is the two-dimensional snapshot of leadership, the action leader must be the holograph. But it's more than that, more even than Indra's net. Because a holograph and Indra's pearls reflect reality. The truth is, you *interact* with reality, not merely reflect it. That interaction is more than communication. It's communion.

the defining past

I've taken this side road into Buddhist metaphysics, quantum mechanics and holographic technology to demonstrate that the fields of experience from which you draw your defining moment and into which you apply it may be more varied, broad and fertile than you have ever imagined. "I believe in eternity," said Emerson. "I can find Greece, Asia, Italy, Spain and the Islands — the genius and creative principle in each and all eras, in my own mind." All of history is in your past, in your mind. Emily Dickinson seldom left her house in Amherst, Mass.; yet the power and range of her poems testify that she lived as exciting a life as Hannibal, Caesar or Napoleon. Emerson said: "What was done in a remote age by men whose names have resounded far, has no more deeper sense than what you do today."

a treasure of defining moments

Not everybody can be a great order leader. It takes a commanding presence and if not an unshakable ego, at least the ability to make an outward display of one. But most people can be action leaders, because you do not have to rely on brittle ego or on authority but instead on a pearl of Indra: you. You are a treasure of defining moments. Here's how you can seek — and find.

recall profound change

Remember an event or events that changed you dramatically. When I speak of your being changed, I do not mean that you became a different person. Our world is sustained by two miracles: the miracle of change and the miracle of permanency. In 1949, physicist Richard Feynman formulated mathematical expressions and diagrams establishing that, moment by moment, subatomic particles are being created and destroyed. The particles even go forward *and* backward in time! Yet each new particle possesses the same, unchanging fundamental characteristics of the particle that was destroyed. This the-more-things-change-the-more-they-stay-the-same miracle of physics finds its correlation with human consciousness and personality. On one hand, our consciousness is a field of dynamic change as, moment by moment, thoughts come and go, are created and annihilated. Yet we know that throughout our lives, our personalities remain fundamentally the same. The 80-year-old is essentially the same person she was as a 3-year-old. Clearly, there are aspects of that person's personality that have changed, that have grown in knowledge, wisdom and awareness. But the fundamental, defining characteristics of that personality, unless distorted by illness or extreme trauma, have remained.

applying the defining moment

Understanding these points will better enable you to understand and apply your defining moment. For you must fix that moment of change within the context of the unchanging you.

Thus the executive asserted that when he raised his hand in the classroom, his life was changed, yet in the same breath, he also said, "That boy was me!"

Better yet, he could have said: "That boy *is* me!" To make the defining moment live now, so it can live for the audience and the audience live for it, you must be that person now who was changed back then, no matter how long ago "back then" was.

Let's start to develop your defining moment.

describe the events

Write down that memory of when you underwent dramatic change.

Use pen, typewriter, word processor or tape recorder/transcriber — whatever suits you best. The important thing: Get it on paper.

Don't analyze what you are putting down. At this stage, take the advice of former Boston Red Sox pitcher "Spaceman" Bill Lee gives ballplayers: "Thinking can be fatal. To stay on top in baseball, you've got to bypass your brain completely so that impulses shoot directly from your eyes to your fingertips. Technically speaking, you must rely on your sympathetic and parasympathic nervous systems."

be a recording instrument

You are at this stage simply a recording instrument for your recollections. Your recollections are not only physical but emotional as well. Don't dwell on the emotions you stir up. You may be tempted to linger on events, especially since the act of putting them on paper often reveals them to you for the first time in years. Freud described psychoanalysis as the "talking cure." This is the "writing cure." Except it is not a cure for psychological problems but for those impediments to your becoming an action leader. You are not trying to come to grips with the memories, simply record them. Get the memory out of your brain, through your fingertips and onto paper as quickly as possible.

The changes might not be tied to a single moment. They might have happened over a period of months or years. We'll deal with compressing it into a single moment shortly.

Furthermore, I am not telling you how much to write. You may want to capture it in a paragraph, a page or a number of pages. I have had leaders in my seminars write down only a few sentences and others warm to the subject and write scores of pages.

describe the change

— Write exactly how those events changed you.

— Write the physical changes that took place. Then write the psychological changes.

— Write the changes that occurred not only with you but with others involved in the situation.

— Write what did *not* change, what remains the same today.

relate to present

With your defining moment roughed out, go back to the answer that you developed concerning what is happening now.

Write three-to-five specific ways in which your defining moment relates to what is happening now. It's essential that the linkages be concrete so that the relationship between the defining moment and what is happening now is clear, compelling and functional.

the connection can always be made

Often, people tell me that they do not know how to make the then-and-now connection. Don't worry; that connection can always be made because it is always there. The very power of the transformation you underwent, no matter how long ago, lives in you today — no exceptions! As two subatomic particles once tuned to each other's spin will always stay in tune, so you are now and will always be intimately engaged with your defining moment. You just have to see the engagement. One way you can see it is ask,

"If that moment did not happen, who, what and where would I be today?" Another way is by bringing the moment into the present. Ask, "What would happen to me today if it happened today?"

boil it down to a moment

Now that you have a rough defining moment or series of events linked to what is happening now, go to the refinement stage.

3. REFINE

There are four aspects to refinement:

a. Pick it out.
b. Flesh it out.
c. Check it out.
b. Condense it.

Few defining moments present themselves, like Venus rising from sea foam, as a complete, perfectly formed moment. But for reasons given in Chapter 4, it is essential that you find the moment in the events. Here are several ways to do it:

—pick it out

Pick the most memorable scene you can think of that took place during the events. Use that as a basis for the moment. Create a composite moment from the events that you remember. It is not important that the moment took place exactly as you state it. You are aiming for emotional truth rather than precise historical truth. In fact, there is no such thing as objective historical truth. History is truly the biography of a madman. Take Kennedy's assassination as an example. There is not one fact concerning the moment of assassination that is not disputed. The good Dr. Johnson again has it right. He said, "If a man could say nothing against a character but what he can prove, history could not be written."

— flesh it out

Your defining moment will not be useful unless you make it brief, clear and powerful. Once you have a defining moment roughed out, flesh it out as fully as possible. (Remember, you are writing the moment now — not the rough experience you initially wrote down.) Flesh it out with facts. You cannot tell somebody to feel an emotion. You can only bring them into an emotion-rich environment and let their feelings well up from inside them. You create that environment by describing the circumstances of the moment. Use all your senses to get the facts of the circumstances; eye, ear, nose, tongue, touch. In other words, what did you see? What did you hear? What did you smell? What did you taste? What did you touch? It is not the facts themselves, it is the impression of the facts upon your mind, that triggers emotion. But without facts, there is no emotion.

the death of Anton Chekhov

Here is a defining moment, the death of the great writer Anton Chekhov in 1904, as told by his wife Olga Knipper.

Gravely ill with tuberculosis in Germany, he sent for a doctor around midnight. To strengthen Chekhov's weak pulse and ease his breathing, the doctor ordered champagne. Olga recalled, "Chekhov sat up and in an emphatic voice said to the doctor in German (of which he knew very little): '*Ich sterbe* . . . '(I'm dying). Then he picked up the glass, turned to me, smiled his wonderful smile and said: 'It's been such a long time since I've had champagne.' He drank it all to the last drop, quietly lay on his left side and was soon silent forever. The awful stillness of the night was broken only by a huge nocturnal moth which kept crashing painfully into the light bulbs and darting about the room. The doctor left and in the stillness and heat of the night the cork flew out of the half-empty champagne bottle with a tremendous noise."

passion is eloquence

Olga wasn't a writer but an actress. She didn't relate this moment with grand literary style but with simplicity and directness. Her emotion was embedded in the facts. Passion is eloquence. We write and speak most eloquently when we forget our ourselves, when we jump headfirst and heartfirst into our task. Paradoxically, when we forget ourselves, we become truly ourselves. We become devoid of vanity and other forms of self-centeredness and exist in the moment of pure feeling and action, a moment that is a pearl of Indra. It is that self, that simple and natural self, which is eloquence itself and which we must strive always to bring to the motivational dance.

— *check it out*

Now that you have your defining moment written from your perspective, write it from the perspectives of other people involved in it. When it is as full, factual and rich in feeling as you can get it, then check it against the characteristics in the previous chapter. It does not have to test out with every characteristic. But if it doesn't, why not? The more characteristics it incorporates, the better chance it has of being effective. Then begin condensing.

— *condense it*

Voltaire said that the secret of being a bore is to tell everything. In developing your defining moment, I want you to tell practically everything — but to yourself, not to your audience. One test of a defining moment is how much good material you leave out.

You don't have to reduce things like the cub reporter who, being told to provide only the essentials in obituaries, wrote, "John Q looked up the elevator shaft to see if the car was coming. Age 36." But you can condense a great deal and that means cutting out deadwood.

— Cut out any character or characters who do not further the point you are making.

— Cut out descriptions that don't help convey emotion.

— Cut out action that doesn't develop the moment.

— Cut out paragraphs, sentences and words that are redundant.

— Cut out everything but the last paragraph or two. Often, the complete defining moment is in that final passage. If the passage doesn't make sense, you can always restore the rest.

THE END IS THE BEGINNING

The development of your defining moment is now complete — but not in the sense that it is hardened into concrete. See it not as rock but as flame that will, over the years, change shapes and throw off varying degrees of light and heat. It may be hidden under a bushel or flicker low or grow tall and strong, as the moment in our executive's speech, to be a bright beacon, illuminating the way for the people you speak to. The moment is never something you have but always something you give. To give something of value, always adapt it to each individual speaking opportunity. We make a living by what we get, but we execute action leadership by what we give.

ACTION TO TAKE:

The answer to the challenge of every speaking situation that calls for action leadership lies in the hearts of your audience. As I said before, they are both the motivators and the motivatees. But it is the action leader's responsibility not only to trigger the audiences' own impulses to motivate themselves but also to give direction and power to the action they take. A powerful way to make that happen is to develop and communicate your defining moment, that moment in your past when you were profoundly moved and changed. I have provided a three-step overview for developing a defining moment. Here is a more detailed way:

1. Understand what is happening now by answering the three needs. What does the audience need? What does the situation need? And what do you, the speaker, need?

2. Recall an event or events that made a dramatic change in your life.

3. Write down your memory of those events to create your defining experience.

4. Make concrete and functional connections between those events and what is happening now.

5. Transform that defining experience into a defining moment by compressing what happened into a moment in time.

6. Flesh out that moment by recalling the physical facts that gave you the powerful emotions.

7. Pare the moment down to two things: one is a one-or-two sentence statement that describes the moment. The other is a one-or-two page narrative.

8. Be prepared to change the moment and the way you describe it to meet each new situation.

7

Defining Moment of the Moment

THERE IS ANOTHER defining moment that must live in your motivational speech. That is *the defining moment of the moment*, the moment when you speak. You must find it, shape it and communicate it. Don't confuse that moment with your personal defining moment. Don't confuse it with what is happening at the moment. Don't confuse it with the audience's need or your vision. It is a separate moment that, through the art of the speech, can live for today and tomorrow. For in seizing it, the words you speak don't die but just begin to live.

the light of the world

John F. Kennedy found and shaped a moment on that cold, bright January day in 1961 when, delivering his inaugural address on the steps of the Capitol, he spoke of the torch being passed to a new generation of Americans and made the "Ask not what you can do for your country . . . . " call to action. That moment found its way into the hearts of countless people across the nation and around the world. Shortly after that speech, I happened to spend a half year in Virginia rooming with a captain in the Chinese Marine Corps who was so taken by the speech that throughout those months, he continually repeated its phrases to me in a heartfelt way, especially the "Ask not . . . " call.

"My defining moment!"

Recently, more than three decades later, I was giving a seminar on the defining moment to MBA students when a Malaysian businessman spoke of listening to that speech as a child over a two-way radio in a jungle village. "That was my defining moment!" he said. "I decided then that even though my family was poor, nothing was going to stop me from getting a university education so I could serve my country."

How many thousands of leaders around the world who heard those words back then made that moment a guiding principle in their lives? Today, the moment lives in their hearts, ideas, programs and actions, and in the people affected by them. And surely the moment will go on, moving men and women yet to be born.

We are not John Kennedys challenging our nation to a higher purpose, but we can all make our own moments work for us in small and large ways. We do that in two ways, by finding the moment or making it.

1. FIND IT

Asked the secret of her joy and serenity, a grand dame I once knew said, "I make the most of what comes — and the least of what goes." That's the secret of finding the defining moment of the moment. You have to make the most of what comes to you. A nugget of a dramatic moment can always be found in the gravel bed of a speaking situation. Pan for it. But know what you're looking for. Know the difference between a pyrite moment and pure gold. Here's a way of assaying the moment's purity.

— *it is simple*

Motivational speech isn't abstract art. It's like a Hollywood movie, a commercial enterprise. It is not a thing of beauty for beauty's sake, or prestige. "Whenever I hear the words 'prestige movie,' " said Louis B. Mayer of MGM studios, "I start losing money." Motivational speech must make money. Since the currency of the speech is action, making money means getting people to act. Like a good, commercial Hollywood movie, it must be simple to understand. It doesn't take a degree in international relations to understand the conflict in Kennedy's speech: the Free World against the Communist World.

— *it is interesting*

"I'm afraid of nothing," said Greta Garbo in the movie, *Camille*, "except being bored." In leadership communication, dull is devastating. If the dramatic moment doesn't interest people, you're wasting your time speaking. Don't speak about the drama of a three-day cricket match to an audience of Chicago Cubs bleacher bums. As Sam Goldwyn said of audiences' reactions to dull movies, "If they don't want to come to the movie, you can't stop them."

— *it is personal*

The moment must be momentous — to you and your audience. A movie audience weeps, gets angry and laughs not because the director had those feelings but because they empathize with the actors and actresses in action. As we saw with our crying policeman in Chapter 3, we do not feel something until we can bring what we see into our hearts. If your audience in some way does not personalize the moment, develop another moment. Kennedy's call to government service was a highly personal charge for thousands of people around the world, challenging them to rethink their values and vision.

— *it is transcending*

Though the moment must be highly personal, it must also connect them with a larger, more important world. Removing a hangnail is a personal not a transcendant experience. Too many leaders focus on the business equivalent of hangnails in speaking. They avoid challenging their audience to commit themselves to a higher purpose in their work. Constantly challenge your dance partners to be more than they think they are and do more than they think they can do. People who make themselves better make others they work with better too. Without those higher purposes of Kennedy's, his challenges would have died aborning on the speaking platform.

2. MAKE IT

Moments are born and made. They shape us and we shape them. They are like the small diamond ring a poor young man gave his fiancee. "I'm sorry," he said, "It's not very big." She replied, "It's as big as we make it." Moments are as big as we make them. We are what we think we'll be. Kennedy shaped the moment in 1961. Lincoln shaped a moment in Gettysburg in 1863. Churchill shaped moments on radio during the Battle of Britain. The moments existed in the drama of the times, but the speakers gave the moments definition, clarity, power and direction.

In shaping the moment, let's look at what everybody else looks at then see something different. Be like Gen. Ferdinand Foch in the Second Battle of the Marne in World War I when he reported, "My center is giving way, my right retreats, situation excellent, I am attacking!"

Now let's go to the payoff: getting people to take the action you want.

8

Action in Leadership

TODAY, THE TRUE word for communication is empowerment and the true word for leadership is motivation. Empowerment and action leadership go hand in hand. Their challenges are the challenges of the motivational speech. They are not new challenges. The motivational speech came into being in Western civilization some 2,500 years ago when the Athenian statesman and lawgiver Solon enabled landless men to vote in the popular assembly and jury trials. That unprecedented act has caused no end of trouble in the world. For it was based on the concept of free speech that is revolutionary today as it was in Solon's time.

ANGRY SOCRATES

Solon's laws established in effect that the man who could motivate others to vote for his cause was superior to the man who couldn't, despite the latter's social status. That precept infuriated Socrates. "The beginning of wisdom," said Socrates, "is in the definition of terms." Socrates railed against the sophists who made a profession of teaching others how to prepare and deliver motivational speeches. The Greek word *sophos* means wise, mentally adroit. But Socrates asserted that the sophists were fools, that they didn't define terms but taught tricks of rhetoric. It was Socrates, through Plato, who gave the word *sophistry* a deceitful twist. In fact, Plato's *Dialogues* were based in one way or another on a seminal conflict that tore at Athens through the fifth and fourth centuries B.C., the conflict between oligarchy and democracy. The motivational speech was an expression of that conflict.

POWERFUL WEAPONS

Socrates was right philosophically but wrong politically. For in giving the vote to the dispossessed, Solon gave them weapons to seize power. Those weapons were words. In fact, as long as free speech reigned in Athens, words, not arms, were the most powerful weapons. Men most skilled in speech became most powerful. Empowerment was speech. To speak was to be empowered. Without free speech, the glory of Athens, her great dramas, her military victories (ancient Greek historian Herodotus said that Marathon was a triumph of free men's spirit), her art, philosophies and politics would not have happened, and Athens would have been a backwater city-state.

ORDER VS. ACTION LEADERSHIP

That conflict of ancient Greece resonates today as order leadership gives way to action leadership. Order leadership is oligarchic, action leadership democratic. Order leadership thrives by keeping information and power (often the same things) centralized in the hands of the few. Action leadership demands that information and power be decentralized in the hands of the many. And when information and power are decentralized, speech-giving becomes paramount. For order leaders, giving speeches is often a nuisance. For action leaders, speech giving is like the air we breathe.

let us march!

Motivational speech must trigger action. The Greek saying that "When Aeschines spoke, they said, 'how well he speaks.' But when Demosthenes spoke, they said, 'Let's march against Philip!' " is not description but a standard to meet. Your speech should get the audience to spring to their feet, wanting to do something specific.

To get people to take action, let's understand the nature and use of action in the motivational speech. For you can trigger both right action and wrong action. Here are characteristics of right action.

1. ACTION IS PHYSICAL

The action your audience is motivated to take should be, for the most part, physical. It is usually not something the audience feels, tastes, thinks, or hears; it is something the audience does, most often with their feet and hands. Many leaders confuse this point. They aim to inspire their audience. But you must do more than inspire. You must motivate. Which means you must get the audience to "motor," to "move."

Inspiration is not motivation. When inspired, you *in*-spire, "inhale the spirit." The word's origins go back to the Oracle of Delphi, the prophesying priestesses of ancient times. The Oracle was called Pythia, and her temple in Greece's Delphi was located on the mythical site where Apollo killed the serpent Python. Pythia was a priestess of Apollo, and she prophesied in an underground chamber of her temple, situated over a fissure in rock that dropped into the bowels of the earth.

inspired knowledge

Noxious vapors reputedly rose out of the fissure. Pythia inhaled or "inspired" the vapors (inhaling in a sense earth-knowledge and spirit), went into a trance and delivered her prophecies. She did not take action. Instead, her prophecies led to action. Pythia predicted that, after the battle of Marathon, when the Persians were preparing to attack Athens again that the Athenians could only be saved by a wall of wood. That wall turned out to be the Greek navy, which defeated the Persian fleet at Salamis. Pythia's inspiration created the motivation to enlarge the Greek fleet.

dissipated emotions

Most of us have heard speakers who are long on inspiration but short on motivation. Their speeches sound better than they actually are. They inspire us, yes, but move us not. Our momentary emotion dissipates quickly after we stop inspiring the speech's magical vapors and have to get on with our work and our lives. Inspired people only get results when they are motivated to take action.

2. ACTION IS PURPOSEFUL

As action leaders, we must live our lives with a sense of mission. Alarm clocks should not wake us in the morning. Purpose should wake us. Action without purpose is a kind of running around in the dark. We must be sure that we invest our audiences with purpose too. They must understand what we are challenging them to do. You might ask, *if they are doing something, don't they understand it?* In many cases, they do not. It's a fallacy that action is truth. People often act without understanding what they are doing. History is replete with people who laid down their lives for wrong ideas.

wrong ideas passionately held

But what are the right ideas? Often, what we think is right is totally wrong. In 1687, a respected London critic said that John Milton's "memory will always stink." Many 17th-century Spanish dukes bankrupted their estates by obsessively accumulating dwarfs, prime collectables of that era. In the late 19th century, a German mathematician spent his career writing an enormous two-volume, unified system of math. Just before the second volume was published, a young British mathematician, Bertrand Russell, posed a question about the system. Because the German could not answer the question, he was forced to publish a postscript to the second volume conceding that both volumes were useless as a unified system. About the same time, the head of the U.S. Patent Office suggested that it be closed because he claimed that "everything that can be invented has been invented." In 1930, the U.S. Department of Labor forecasted 1930 to be a "splendid employment year." In 1957, an editor of a New York publishing firm turned down a manuscript on the recently developed science of data processing by saying, "I can assure you on highest authority that data processing is a fad and won't last out the year."

The list of wrong views carefully reasoned and passionately held is endless. But that is no excuse for us to succumb to paralysis-by-analysis. The don't-do-something-just-stand-there! call to non-action is an affliction too. Often, we don't know what we have until we use it, and we don't know what we are until we undergo trial-by-action. But our action can be most effective when it is undertaken with clear purpose.

three impulses to purpose

Purpose in the motivational speech has three aspects: reason, feeling and awareness. Don't motivate people to take action unless you and they understand what action they need to take. The Light Brigade's purpose ". . . not to reason why but to do or die!" is a slavery of will. But though action must spring from the hardpan of reason, it takes wings through feelings and dreams. Poet Langston Hughes wrote, "Don't let your dream die. Without a dream, life like a bird with a broken wing cannot fly."

Finally, your audience must know of the "flight," the action being taken. If I have motivated an audience to pick up their left foot and set it down in front of their right foot (and in terms of motivational speeches, this specific kind of action is best), then the audience must understand clearly that they are picking up their left foot and setting it down in front of their right foot. They must know that they are doing it *as they are doing it* and know why they are doing it.

3. ACTION IS HONESTY

A motivational dance is a lever that can move the world, but dishonesty or trickery on the part of either party can snap that lever. Socrates was wrong politically but wrong in a larger not smaller sense. If, without democracy and free speech — and that meant having the freedom to utter "sophistries" — Athens would not have been distinguished in history, the fact still remains that the Athenian sophists did engage in the teaching of rhetorical trickery, and in that sense Socrates was right. Speech is given to trickery. You cannot buy the Brooklyn Bridge for a nickel from a silent man.

But speech not only is given to trickery, it *is* trickery. There is an element of cosmic hoax in the fact that when person A moves muscles that resonate his vocal cords and shapes exhalations with teeth, tongue, lips and jaws to make air disturbances which vibrate the eardrums of person B, then person B may leap upon person A and, depending upon what pattern of chemical firings race through B's brain, either kiss person A with passion or murder him in cold blood. "Mankind's own peculiar condition," said Montaigne, "is that we are fit to be laughed at as able to laugh." Yet Montaigne and other great sages who acknowledge the comedy of humans also challenge people to find meaning in life's absurdity by caring for others. We cannot care for others without honoring them. And we cannot honor others unless we first honor ourselves. To honor ourselves is to be honest with ourselves and with others.

the Groucho Marx test

Though Diogenes, carrying a lantern through the streets of Corinth, searched diligently, and supposedly unsuccessfully, for an honest man, Groucho Marx had an easier test: "Ask him if he's honest," said Groucho. "If he says, 'yes,' he's crooked." Easily mocked because it is easily mouthed ("The more honest he said he was," said Emerson of an acquaintance, "the more we counted our spoons."), honesty is nonetheless the gold standard of the dance. We cannot motivate without being honest and speaking honestly. I'm not just talking about law-abiding honesty. Often, profoundly honest people are lawbreakers, as witnessed by the history of the Quakers and by the U.S. Civil Rights movement in the 1950s and '60s. I'm talking about honesty of character. We know it when we see it. Better yet, we know it when it affects us.

a metaphor of need

Honesty has nothing to do with institutions. Our jails, I'm sure, contain many inmates of truly honest character, while the boards and the pulpits of churches and the offices of moral agencies contain many people with truly dishonest character. Honesty of character has nothing to do with people's looks, presence, intelligence and way with words. Handsome, poised and articulate people can prove to be distrustful, just as ugly, awkward people can prove trustful. Finding honest character is vital to us. Diogenes' search is a metaphor for human need. Being social creatures, needing to trust people, to commune with people, we walk the darkling plains of life, day in and day out, lanterns outstretched, asking Groucho's question, "Are you honest?" If people do not believe that you are being honest with them, you may give them orders from here to eternity but will never motivate them.

Worst of all, if you betrayed their trust by getting them to act through deception, they'll regret that action, and regret and remember having dealt with you for a long, long time.

the Checkers Speech

Many people were taken in by Richard Nixon's "sophistries" in his famous "Checkers Speech." In the presidential campaign of 1952, the disclosure of an $18,000 private slush fund created on his behalf by California millionaires threatened to terminate Nixon's political career. Nixon was Dwight Eisenhower's vice-presidential candidate on the Republican ticket, and many party leaders urged Eisenhower to get a new running mate. Eisenhower, an American hero who promised to bring the troops home from the Korean War, waffled. Nixon persuaded the Republican National Committee to buy television time immediately after comedian Milton Berle's top-rated show. In the speech, Nixon didn't "define the terms." In fact, he made up his own terms. He didn't deny the existence of the slush fund. He couldn't. It was in the open. Instead, Nixon talked about growing up poor, being in World War II and fighting communism. He said that his wife Pat "... doesn't have a mink coat but a respectable Republican cloth coat."

Checkers

He concluded by saying that he had to make one more confession or " . . . they'll probably be saying this about me too. We did get something, a gift after the election. A man down in Texas heard Pat on the radio mention the fact that our two youngsters would like to have a dog. And, believe it or not, the day before we left on this campaign trip, we got a message from Union Station in Baltimore saying that they had a package for us. We went down to get it. You know what it was? It was a little cocker-spaniel dog in a crate that he had sent all the way from Texas. Black-and white-spotted. And our little girl Tricia, the 6-year-old, named it Checkers. And you know, the kids love the dog, and I just want to say this right now, that regardless of what they say about it, we're gonna keep it!"

Nixon prevails

The general public supported Nixon. Eisenhower didn't dump him. Nixon's political career wasn't over; it was just beginning.

Yet as the evasions and rhetorical tricks used in that speech began to sink into the public's consciousness, Nixon got the sobriquet he could never shake, "Tricky Dick."

national nervous breakdown

Nixon's presidency contributed to our nation's people being divided against each other. Flyers showing Nixon's jowly, scowling face and the words, "Would you buy a used car from this man?" with the implicit message, *You can't trust him!*, was more than political doggerel; it was a "laughing-to-keep-from-crying" cry of pain. With the nation embroiled in the Vietnam War, people badly needed leadership that would help knit the country together.

They needed a common, compelling vision. Nixon's leadership tore the country apart, not because he espoused extreme political views (in retrospect, he was a rather moderate conservative) but because he displayed extreme leadership deficiencies: People simply felt that he was not being honest with them. Laboratory animals often become neurotic when their freedom of choice is removed. When you have power over people and lie to them and they know that you are lying, you diminish their power to make free choices. Because so many people felt they were being lied to by Nixon, Lyndon B. Johnson and many other government officials, people believed that they could not affect the course of government. The nation underwent a kind of nervous breakdown during the late 1960s and early '70s, with assassinations, urban riots, campus upheavals and race hatreds rampant.

Lincoln and Nixon

Heaven or hell can flow from our hearts; and if we are leaders, that heartflow can make a heaven or hell of the lives of the people we lead. Clearly, the ills of our society cannot be traced to the outflowings of Nixon's heart. Leaders must always play with the cards dealt them. The deepest and most persistent contradictions of racial hatreds, poverty and governmental deceit had been festering in our society long before he came to office. When he was elected in 1968 at the height of the Vietnam War, he was dealt an appalling hand. We will misunderstand Nixon if we don't have compassion for him and his plight. Still, leadership tells. It tells in the marketplace, however we define that marketplace. Another leader, playing with the same cards, might have started to heal the nation's wounds rather than open them. I see Lincoln in Nixon's place but not Nixon in Lincoln's place. A leader at war with himself may create wars within the audiences he speaks to. Greedy, selfish, angry leaders can very well increase the sum of greed, selfishness and anger in the people they lead. Action leaders can be so much more effective in the marketplace than order leaders; for in the necessity of the dance, action leaders must speak and act from the honesty of their hearts to the best of their audiences' hearts, and thus get the best out of those audiences.

compassionate conviction

Not being honest with your audience is the shot in the water line of leadership, imperiling order leaders but especially action leaders, who depend on emotional trust.

Here are ways to make sure you are being honest in the dance:

— Focus as always on your audience's needs. See your leadership as bestowing rewards upon your audience, not you. Dishonesty comes from selfishness and greed. Honesty comes from *selflessness* and *compassion.* Focus on serving your audience, and you'll have the best chance of dealing honestly with them.

— Speak from strong conviction. Strength of conviction is good, though not foolproof, evidence that you're being honest with yourself and others. Strength of *compassionate conviction* is the best evidence of all.

4. ACTION GIVES MEANING TO EMOTION

Bring powerful emotion into the dance, but make sure it prompts action. Emotion is the horse that pulls the cart of action leadership. Don't mistake the horse for the cart. The cart is the audience taking action. Without the horse, we may get the cart to move in other ways. But without the cart, the horse is nothing but a bag for hay and water. Action gives the emotion of the defining moment meaning. Without action, the emotion in your dance is nothing more than a "feelie" drug. Humans need to experience powerful emotions. "Make me cry. Make me laugh. Make me fearful. Make me angry." are constant and natural desires that make wealthy and famous the people who can fulfill them. Novelists, playwrights, producers, actors and actresses, screen-writers, and directors, are all in the "make me feel" business. When emotion is sufficient, we have drama and art. When emotion is not sufficient, when it is only given meaning through action, we have action leadership.

5. ACTION IS NEED

Action leadership is not only about action but direction. In a recent high-school basketball game, one team got the ball with four minutes remaining. They were down by 1 point. The coach called a time out and told them to go into a four-corner stall for the rest of the game. During the time out, he spent most of the time explaining how to stall. As they filed back onto the court, he said, "Take the last shot of the game. Don't shoot until five seconds or less remain on the clock." The team spread out and passed the ball while the clock ran down. Finally, five seconds remained. Then four. Then three. Nobody shot! They had gotten into a stall mode. Every player was afraid to put the ball up. The clock ran out. The buzzer sounded. The game was over. They lost by 1 point. After the game, the opposing coach said, "That was the best stall ever accomplished for *my* team!" The losing coach had communicated clear direction about the stall — but not the true need, the need to take a shot and win. Motivate audiences to act by communicating clear direction grounded in their true need. Action *is* need.

6. ACTION IS VISION

Vision in leadership is a higher order of seeing. It is seeing things and also seeing into things, around things and through things. The more you see not through the faculty of sight but through imagination and spirit, the more you can challenge your audience to do. We'll examine vision and action leadership in the next chapter.

7. ACTION IS COMMITMENT

I came of age in the days of the military draft. If you were healthy and weren't married or in school, you either had to enlist or were drafted. Most draftees and even most enlistees I knew were not eager to go and not particularly happy to be in. But today, looking back, many say that they are grateful that they went. In the military, they learned firsthand in many interesting ways that military intelligence is often an oxymoron. They were forced to undergo experiences that ultimately enlarged and defined their lives. "A kick in the seat of the pants," said David Sarnoff, founder of NBC, "gets you farther along in life than a pat on the back."

Sometimes people need a "kick in the seat of the pants," metaphorically, of course, to get them moving. Often, in that action they discover talents and commitments they do not know they have and get experiences they might not otherwise obtain.

8. ACTION IS SMALL IN SCOPE

Many leaders who want to motivate people to go to the mountain, will say in effect, "let's go to the mountain!" — even though the mountain be halfway 'round the world. Action is most effective when specific and small in scope. Let's not try to do everything at once, but do something at once. Challenge them to do something specific immediately. You may want them to go to the mountain, but motivate them first to buy good hiking boots, knowing and making sure that they know that the purchase is, in effect, going to the mountain.

9. ACTION IS TRANSFORMATION

In action, we transform our needs and beliefs. We can change the world only when we change ourselves, and often we are changed most profoundly when we do something. By what we do today, we transform the future long before it happens. In *Walden*, Thoreau said, "I was determined to know beans." He did not read books about beans but instead *hoed beans*, in bean season, from 5 a.m. to noon, and grew to know beans: their costs; their income; their buyers; their weed companions; their seeds; their needs; the weather that nourished them; the woodchucks that ate them; the soil, mixed with artifacts and ashes of bygone American Indian camps, that sustained them; the men who commented upon them; their taste in his mouth; the ideas that came to mind while he hoed. With hoe in hand, feet in the soil and sweat on his brow, Thoreau was transformed in his needs and beliefs by knowing beans, and thus, through the publication of *Walden*, transformed the world.

As action leaders, we all must be determined to test and nourish our needs and beliefs and those of our dance partners by dancing. Get your audience doing something, and you'll always get them, and you, needing and believing something new. Sweep away doubts with deeds.

ACTION TO TAKE:

Before you challenge an audience to take action, answer:

— What is the clear purpose of that action?

— What physical action will they take?

— What do you feel deeply about in regard to that action?

— What is the meaning your audience's action gives to your defining moment?

— What is your vision that prompts the audience to take action?

— What are the audience's needs and beliefs that will change through the action they take?

— How can you make their action specific?

— What greater goal is their specific action leading to?

— Are they aware of that goal? If not, why not? If so, is it the goal you want them to be aware of?

9

Action From Vision

HERE'S A LESSON in vision. Go down to your basement and look at the floor joists. Are the largest edge-knots located on the upper side of the joists? Are the joists doubled under all parallel bearing partition walls? Is cross-bridging used between the joists? If so, a visionary carpenter was at work.

The upper-side knots are on the compression side of the member. Double joists under parallel bearing partition walls give added weight-bearing protection. Cross-bridging provides added support for joists and supporting partitions above them.

In many cases, these details are not required by code. But the carpenter, knowing it or not, has communicated a vision of being willing to go beyond what is minimally required.

On the other hand, a carpenter who uses 6-inch joists instead of 10-inch joists, who doesn't double the joists under the bearing partition walls, and who neglects cross-bridging or solid bridging between the joists has communicated a vision that less-is-OK.

Vision is everywhere, in the shoes we buy, the clothes we wear, the food we eat, the service we get at a check-out counter. The trouble is, most vision in this world is both unintended and flawed.

flawed vision

Flawed vision, intended or not, can cause more trouble than most leadership deficiencies. The flawed vision of the North that the South could be quickly and relatively easily defeated ("The rebels, a mere band of ragamuffins," wrote a Philadelphia editor, "will fly before our approach like chaff before wind.") was shattered by the defeat of Union troops at the Battle of Bull Run. In the confusion of that defeat, many Northern leaders tried to sue for peace. The flawed vision of the Big Three that the Japanese automakers could not effectively compete resulted in Detroit's responding ineffectually to Japanese competition in the '70s and '80s. The examples of the pernicious consequences of flawed vision are countless.

be aware of your vision

The combination of the defining moment and vision is the ideology of action leadership. Without a clear, compelling vision, any task, whether hoeing beans or marketing biotechnological products, becomes a bore. Without that vision, the music gets out of rhythm and the dancers step on each other's toes. That ideology begins in awareness. I don't care if you lead one person, 1,000 people or 100,000 people, you must, as an action leader, have intended vision. Be mindful of what that vision is and what it is perceived to be. Eliminate its flaws. Amplify and refine it. Communicate it skillfully. Have your audience take action through it.

Here are nine aspects of vision:

1. VISION BEGINS WITH YOU

Speech begins with the audience and their needs, but vision begins with you. You cannot find it in your audience but must look for it instead in your heart. If vision is a higher order of seeing, it is born in a higher order of living, in your profound life experiences. If you have not in some way lived it intensely, your audience cannot experience it. And if they can't experience it and take action out of that experience, it is useless to you and to them.

vision is not a defining moment

However, don't mistake your vision for your defining moment. They are two separate action-leadership tools, and your audience should know they are separate. The defining moment brings you into an emotional relationship with your audience; vision points the way that relationship should go. The defining moment is ballast; vision is sail and compass. A vision comes from a defining moment.

A defining moment doesn't come from vision. Our sales executive in Chapter 4 told his sales force of his defining moment when he raised his hand. But that wasn't his vision. His vision came from that experience. His vision was, "I don't have a job, I have a vow!" and by extension, "Your job must be a vow too!" A defining moment is the dramatic narrative of your being changed. A vision is the lesson you draw from that narrative or experience, a lesson that is transmuted into a powerful expectation of what may come to be. Once you have developed that vision, you can apply it to the other side of the motivational equation: the audience.

2. IT MUST BE GROUNDED IN FACTS

In 1783, French peasants laboring in fields saw the devil descending from the heavens. They attacked it with pitchforks, attached it to horses and ripped it to shreds having it dragged across the countryside. But the creature wasn't the devil; it was one of the first balloons ever made, a helium-filled bag of rubberized silk, released by faraway strangers. The peasants' vision of the devil-come-to-earth did not square with the facts of the situation. Vision must be based on facts, not facts on vision. Without facts, vision itself becomes an untethered balloon blown hither and yon. When Montgomery spoke to his Eighth Army staff for the first time (See Chapter 2) and told them that withdrawal was no longer an option (thus communicating a new vision to troops who had been constantly retreating), he spoke not only of what they were going to do but how they would do it. He spoke of the detailed staff work that lay ahead, of sending transportation to the rear and bringing ammunition, water, rations, etc., to the forward positions, of bringing new troops up to reinforce them, of forming a new armor corps from the bits and pieces of divisions that had been fighting scattered all over the desert.

vision and defining moment

Likewise, our sales leader's vision of vow in his speech in Chapter 4 was backed by his three decades of experience in business and by his detailing three fundamental marketing flaws that the competition was making. Your vision must come from the facts of your defining moment and from the facts of your working experience.

You don't have to work decades before you can develop a vision. Many of you are just starting your jobs or have changed jobs or even gone into a new field of work. But no matter how new — or old — you are to the job, you must always create your vision from a powerful perception of the facts at hand and of your life.

3. IT MUST BE CLEAR, SIMPLE, AND BRIEF

"If the laws of physics weren't simple," said Einstein, "I

wouldn't be interested in them." Many of Einstein's great concepts were developed not through complex mathematics but through his envisioning simple, concrete pictures.

His special theory of relativity was based on the question that had aroused his curiosity since childhood, "What would a beam of light look like if I am going as fast as it goes?" His general theory of relativity came to him while he was working in a patent office in 1907. He called it "The happiest idea of my life . . . . If a man falls freely, he will not feel his own weight." This thought propelled him to the theory of gravitation.

Often, Einstein developed a picture, a vision, in his mind, that was simple enough for the public to understand, and only later tested its truth through equations. "Imagination," he said, "is more important than knowledge."

higher order of being

Though vision is a higher order of seeing, it must be as simple and concrete as Thoreau's "knowing by hoeing." It must be simple because it is a trigger for action. It must be concrete because it must always be compelling. The average fourth-grader should understand it immediately and it should be concise enough to be written on the back of a business card.

4. IT MUST BE TIED TO YOUR DEFINING MOMENT

Though a vision begins with you, it must end with the audience. If it does not help the audience take action and give purpose and direction to that action, drop it. To get action, vision must be fresh and challenging.

My experience confirms that leaders make two common mistakes in regard to vision. Either we have not given thought to having a vision and so have an unintended vision (which is usually a flawed vision), or we have developed a hackneyed vision. Such visions as "Getting paychecks to my employees," "Serving the customer," "Making it easy to do business with us," "Being number one in the customer's estimation" are hackneyed visions. You'll get people as enthusiastic about them as you would by declaiming that "The sky is blue!" To be compelling, a vision must be fresh. We are not motivated by trite expressions. However, all the great truths of this world are old truths, truths too important to be new. In vision, old truths must be animated by fresh experience. Insure that it is fresh by grounding it in your defining moment. Out of the uniqueness of that moment comes a unique vision. How do you get that vision from the moment?

It's this: *Vision is the lesson learned from the defining moment.*

In other words, begin to develop your vision this way, "*From my defining moment, I learned . . .* (fill in the blank)."

5. IT MUST PROPEL THE AUDIENCE.

The lesson alone is not good enough. You have one more step to go. You must transform that lesson into a *challenging* expectation for the future.

Action leadership is not about what is comfortable and convenient. It's about change and challenge. If the dancers are not challenging each other, not being changed by dancing, they dance ineffectively.

Montgomery said, "Some think that morale is best sustained when (soldiers are) . . . surrounded by clubs, canteens, and so on. I disagree. My experience with soldiers is that they are at their best when they are asked to face up to hard conditions. Men dumped in some out-of-the-way-spot in the desert will complain less of boredom, because they have to shift for themselves, than those surrounded by a wide choice of amenities."

So the guide to developing a vision is: *From my defining moment I learned* (fill in the blank) *and from that lesson I expect us to be challenged to* (fill in the blank).

6. IT MUST BRING THE FUTURE INTO THE PRESENT

Though vision holds an expectation for the future, it must give impetus to present action. The defining moment is the past at work in the present. Vision is the future at work in the present. You have the power and the freedom to make it work. In action leadership, a vision is not only an expectation or goal but more importantly, the future itself, entering the dancers and being transformed by them and their dance, before that future happens. Action leadership is about freedom, freedom of the dancers to choose, to act from those choices. Vision *is* action, the future in action now.

When our leader challenged his sales force to make their job a vow, he was creating a new vision of selling in which they could take action. It was a vision of the future — a sales force being unmatched in the marketplace because they were bringing an unusually powerful commitment to their tasks. To make that future happen, they had to make that vow take place now.

7. IT MUST BE FELT

Often, the power of vision resides in its *not* being clearly seen and defined in objective terms. Some of the most powerful visions of leaders in history were seen not with the eyes but felt with the heart. The Israelis wandering in Sinai could not objectively see The Promised Land except in their imaginations. The power of that vision was not so much connected with the objective details of a land of milk and honey as with the transforming concepts, the transforming vision, of "land promised" by their God. That ancient vision lives in Western culture as a kind of eternal-liberation theology.

wrong conventional wisdom

I wrote a book about a man who has been a highly successful entrepreneur in mining and petroleum exploration for more than 50 years. A key attribute of his success was his knack for developing a compelling vision for his company. On a number of occasions throughout his career, he saw things that other people did not see and, sometimes against the advice of the "experts" of the day, led the people of his company to seize that vision. For instance, in the early 1960s, he sold most of the assets of his company to embark in what was then a highly risky venture: offshore oil drilling in the Gulf of Mexico. Some oil analysts thought he was half mad to sell proven assets for an unproven enterprise. In fact, in the 1960s, investing in offshore exploration, his company lost money four straight years. But he said that a lifetime experience in oil exploration convinced him that he was right and conventional wisdom wrong. He persisted, and in the end his vision that the Gulf was to be the next boom paid off, and his company participated in that boom.

a vision must be wrong

If your vision is wrong, it's right. Anyone can see things that other people can see, but you become visionary when you see what others don't and open yourself to criticism. Most great advances in human history were at first deemed impossible. Most great ideas start as heresies then end as clichés. Your job as a visionary leader is to get in on the heresy phase. By the time you get in on the cliché or conventional-wisdom phase, you're floating along the dead-fish way, with the stream of things.

8. IT MUST COME FROM THE INDIVIDUAL HEART

A team doesn't create a vision for their individual; an individual creates a vision for the team. This conflicts with today's trend of team building through consensus, a trend grounded to a great extent in Japanese business techniques. Most Westerners have viewed Japan's business success within the context of economics. But it is a superficial way of viewing that success. To truly understand their industrial advances, what they can teach us, but also what we cannot be taught, we must view them in terms of their Confucian/Buddhist/Shinto culture. Japan is the first non-Western, non-Christian culture to excel in industrial competitiveness. Their competitive values and mandates flow from religious roots. Leading Japanese corporations have Shinto shrines at their manufacturing sites, branches and headquarters. Confucian principles and mandates of hierarchy and patriarchy are embedded in the social texture. Many Japanese leaders espouse Buddhist/Shinto precepts as part of their business philosophies. The code of the Samurai warrior, so important to Japan's competitive ethic, is based largely on Buddhist and Zen Buddhist views.

harmony vs. conflict

Asian religions describe a world in which man is one with nature and no more important than sentient creatures, rocks, trees, forefathers and sky. Landscape paintings by Asian artists show human figures as insignificant entities against mountain vastness. Christianity, on the other hand, teaches that man has dominion over nature and that we will be intimately connected with our forbears only after Judgment Day. The former views are certainly not exclusively Japanese. Originating in Buddhism and Taoism, they are prevalent throughout Asia. The views can be boiled down to this fundamental concept: *Success is a function of harmony.* Our Western views, by contrast, argue that success is a function of conflict.

In the West if two business people agree, one is irrelevant. In the East, two business people are not relevant until they agree.

divine conflict

By giving the vote to commoners, Solon empowered the individual. Subsequent generations of Greeks glorified individuality and its fruit, conflict. It was primarily through conflict, not harmony, that individuals advanced politically, economically and artistically. In fact, in conflict, the Greeks glimpsed the divine. Their literature, oratory and rhetoric had their beginnings in the violent conflicts of the *Iliad* and *Odyssey.* Their mythologies were shaped and impassioned by conflicts between gods and gods and humans and gods. Their theater, projected through conflict, was made pre-eminent in their society. (The first structure to be laid out whenever a new Greek city-state was founded was the theater.) It is this glorification of individuality and conflict that imbues Western culture.

companion of sedition

Writing nearly seven centuries later, Roman historian Tacitus asserted that conflict shaped great oratory. "The great and famous eloquence of old is the nursling of the license which fools call freedom. It is the companion of sedition, the stimulant of an unruly people, a stranger to obedience and subjection, a defiant, reckless, presumptuous thing that does not show itself in a well-governed state . . . . Could a community be found in which no one did wrong, an orator would be as superfluous among its innocent people as a physician among the healthy."

divine harmony

But in Asia, conflict is anathema. For thousands of years, the highest forms of Chinese poetry exemplified harmony. The Chinese had their theater and conflict in theater, but it was considered a lower order of expression, relegated to street shows, with a status often below prostitution.

"Empty yourself of everything," said the great Chinese sage, Lao-tzu, "Let the mind rest in peace." To be at peace is to be (not to be in), but to actually *be* "the stream of the universe." Individuals must not stand out. Each individual's essence is in the All, not one. If you are ignorant and foolish enough to stand out individually, you must be planed down flat, made harmonious, so as not to be distinguished from the level grain of things. This submerging and dissipating of your individual self was not for society's sake but your own, enabling you to live a full and meaningful life. As Lao tzu says:

> *On tiptoes, you're not steady.*
> *Moving quickly, you can't walk well.*
> *Pointing to yourself, you are not enlightened.*
> *Bragging, you achieve nothing.*

A far cry from the Greeks' "Man is the measure of all things." Lao-tzu might say, "Man can only be measured *in* all things." Or even better: "Man can only be measured *as* all things."

breaking up the ego

Today, many Western businesses make a mistake trying to make people who have grown up steeped in the European and American celebration of individuality into people who suppress their individuality for the good of the group. That is why so many team and consensus approaches blunder in business today. Such approaches work in theory but not in practice. For Western people to suppress their individuality, they must undergo a kind of imposed neurosis, break their ego apart and re-form it in a totally new way. A species of red sponge can do that. Force that sponge through a strainer and the sponge's protoplasm shatters into thousands of pieces, pieces that re-form themselves on the other side. The reconstituted sponge then lives on as if nothing had happened. But we can't do that so easily with ego. Break it apart, and it does not reconstitute in the original form. It often is rendered dysfunctional. That's why most Asian viewpoints that are grafted upon the body of Western organizations are rejected by powerful cultural antibodies. There is a difference between West and East. And in terms of action leadership, *viva la difference !*

psychology of the juvenile delinquent

There are few park statues devoted to committees. Powerful vision comes from individuals, not teams or committees. The West has a distinct advantage in its ability to develop entrepreneurs. A psychiatrist said, "To understand the psychology of the entrepreneur, you must understand the psychology of the juvenile delinquent." The entrepreneur, like the juvenile delinquent, is restless, dissatisfied, an enemy of convention, the person who flips the blackboard, causes the class to go into turmoil and the teacher to get a black eye! And the vision of the action leader comes from that same dissatisfaction, that same need to turn things upside down.

a fusion of East and West

Yet it would be a mistake to think that action leadership is a product of and can only function in Western culture. Instead, I see action leadership as a *fusion* of both Eastern and Western viewpoints. As leaders we are interdependent, not outside of things but in all and of all things; yet each person's vision is *independent*—

seeing individually anew, lighting up a team, a job, a business, an industry and even the world.

9. VISION IS NOT ONE BUT SEVERAL

Having one vision is not enough to make full use of vision's power. You must hold in your mind and heart several visions. You must have a vision of your specific job, whether you are a supervisor or a CEO; a vision of your business; and a vision of your industry.

a Marine problem in the Drug Corps

The neurosis of our society that I spoke about in the last chapter infected the military. During the early 1970s, the Marine Corps was racked by drugs, racial divisions, and attacks against authority — afflictions that were prevalent in society at large. Many Marines feared that the problems might cause the Corps to be disbanded.

An NCO told me: "Drugs were so widespread that there was a saying that 'You don't have a drug problem in the Marine Corps, but a Marine problem in the Drug Corps.' "

"The only thing I was sure about," said one officer who commanded a truck company, "was that I wasn't on drugs."

Racial beatings became commonplace. Gangs of whites and blacks hunted each other on and off the base at night. An acquaintance of mine, an executive officer of an infantry battalion at that time, said that the muggings and vigilante beatings around his base became so prevalent that he and his commanding officer often spent hours hiding in bushes near the spots where most beatings took place, waiting in ambush with clubs in their hands for the perpetrators.

to hell in a handbasket

Ships and combat units were pulled off line because of racial strife. On some bases, buildings were taken over by black nationalist groups. Senior NCOs and officers, white and black, would not set foot there. And there were many places that black Marines would never dare tread as well, as white supremacist groups proliferated.

Seeing the Corps disintegrating before their very eyes, many leaders quit or retired early.

Yet many stayed, and, in staying, forged a personal vision of their immediate job.

An officer said to me, "I was a platoon commander then. The Corps was going to hell in a handbasket. I couldn't do anything about that. I could only make my platoon the best I could. *I had a private vision of what was right, and I stuck to that vision.*" (Italics mine.)

"you're not in my Corps anymore."

Another said, "In 1971, I commanded a battalion landing team and later a regiment in the 2nd Marine Division. It was not uncommon to have as many as four or five hundred people in a regiment in some form of unauthorized leave. Can you imagine that? Three or four thousand not where they are supposed to be in the 2nd Marine Division in 1971! So we started weeding them out. As far as I'm concerned, you take drugs, you're wounded in action. I don't run a democracy. I help defend it. Quality young people want to be motivated and challenged. They don't want to live in the barracks along side of riffraff. I wanted the riffraff out. No percentages. I cleaned them out. I told them, if you take drugs in my outfit, you're going to go and the band isn't going to play. You're going to get discharged with the kind you should have — non-negotiable."

A few years later, he became commanding officer of the 2nd Marine Division. He said, "Five thousand Marines departed the 2nd Marine Division during the three years and three months that I was privileged to be their leader. I don't know if they're working, but they're not in my Corps anymore. I would rather go to war any day with ten or twelve thousand instead of eighteen thousand if I didn't have to look over my shoulder. I would've thrown five thousand more out if that's what it took. That doesn't mean that we didn't give some of them second chances. Most of the time it didn't work out. Nine of the ten we gave a second chance to screwed up anyway. But I don't regret giving them second chances. You've got to take chances on people. You win wars by gambling."

individual vision

The Marine Corps was turned around not by a single person with a kind of Churchillian overarching vision but by many leaders from corporals to generals creating and putting into action their individual visions of their particular jobs.

ACTION TO TAKE:

"Every revolution," said Emerson, "was once just a thought in one person's mind." We can't do anything important unless we first dream. Powerful vision leads to powerful action. Action leadership must have vision. Here are ways to develop your own powerful vision as an action leader.

— Search for your vision by searching your own heart. You will not find your vision anywhere else. Your vision is personal and emotional.

— Make sure your vision is fresh and challenging. To do that, link it to your defining moment.

— List three-to-five hard facts which will ground your vision in objective reality.

— Boil it down to its essentials — i.e., "We don't have a job, we have a vow!" — so it is concise enough be written on the back of a business card.

— Describe three concrete ways in which your vision of change and challenge for the future can be put into action in the present.

— Describe what your vision sees that is new to your audience.

— Create separate visions: one each for your job, your business and your industry.

10

The Call to Action

THE CALL TO action is a moment of truth in the dance. It is not *the* moment of truth, for there is no single moment in the whole dance, since its essence is activity, but the call is important enough for us to analyze carefully, develop skillfully and use effectively.

WHAT IS THE CALL?

The call to action, like a stellar black hole, is a small, self-contained universe. Like a black hole, where conventional physics is crushed by colossal gravitational forces, the call is where radical transformation takes place. Into it pours the totality of the dancers' pasts; out of it flows action. To begin to understand what the call is, it's important to understand what it is *not.*

the call is not a behavioral technique

During the past several decades, leadership has had an unfortunate association with behavioral psychology. Developed to a great extent in the 1930s through the work of Harvard psychologist B.F. Skinner, behaviorism asserts that psychological studies can only be made by analyzing the objective facts of animal activity. In behavioral terms, animals are what they do. The discipline introduced a refreshing and functional objectivity into a field of study that had been mired in subjective analysis. But behaviorism's premise when applied to leadership, *controlling the consequences of behavior, enables you to control behavior itself,* leads to jargon, strategies and programs designed to produce "appropriate" behavior. It defines leadership relationships not through experience but technique, not through personal commitment but observation, not through trust but power and manipulation. When you lead by controlling people's behavior through the manipulation of their environment, you engage them less on a human than on a clinical level, no matter how much you couch that engagement in such terms as empowerment and team building.

quality is not quantity

Action leadership recognizes that people cannot be defined simply by what they do. Each person brings to the dance a universe of experience. Reality is not just action; it is also actor and actress. The quality of action leadership transcends quantitative analysis. Action leaders do not manipulate relationships, they *experience* relationships. That experience cannot be monitored, measured and shaped by numbers. The word *experience* comes from the Latin root meaning to try or test in peril. Every experience is a kind of trial and involves peril. When you experience relationships, you take risks, you give of yourself in a way that cannot be objectified. As author Ray Bradbury said about writing, "You must jump off a cliff and make your wings on the way down."

a call is not a close

It's often been said that the call to action is like the close of the sale. When selling, you are persuading somebody to make an exchange, to give up one thing for another thing, to pay a price. The close is when you actually get that person to pay the price. In selling, there is no lack of supply, there is only price. Even free inducements come with a price. A great salesman said to me, "Make sure you always get something for your giveaways." Because salespeople must persuade customers to pay a price, the sales people must control the selling situation. Giving the customer control leads to failure, since the customer wants to lower or avoid paying the price altogether.

Action leadership is not salesmanship. The dance is a sales situation minus price. You are not trying to get somebody to give you something. You are trying to get somebody to give themselves something. The dance is not an exchange relationship but an investment relationship. Certainly, you must pay a price to invest in yourself, you must pay a price to take any kind of action, but exchange price is not investment price. When you pay exchange price, the salesperson is usually in control. When you pay investment price, you yourself are usually in control.

a call is not an order

As the call is not a close, so it is not an order. The power of action leadership lies in freedom. You cannot say to the people you lead, as Sam Goldwyn said, "I don't want any yes-men around me — even if it costs them their jobs!" without running the risk of being perceived as an action leader in name only. A visionary executive in a world-leading high-margin, high-value materials business once said to me, "The greatest danger to our business doesn't come from competitors but from letting ourselves become a commodity business while still calling ourselves a high-value business." Likewise, the greatest danger to action leaders is to talk action leadership but *walk* order leadership.

going to the mountain

The leader who wants people to go to the mountain has a tendency to order, "Go to the mountain!" It's only natural to do so. There are the people. There is the mountain. You want them there, so, ostensibly, the easiest way is to tell them to go, or *sell* them on going. In any case, what difference does it make how they got there as long as they get there? It makes all the difference in the world! Leadership, whether order or action, is not a destination but a journey. You are a leader every day of your career. Every day there is a mountain to go to. Often when people are ordered to do something, their action is self-limiting. It stops at and is bounded by the exigencies of the order. Yet the journey goes on — if only in their hearts and minds. They may be angry about being forced to go or may think they were tricked or may be waiting, reluctantly, for the next order. When you tell them to go to the next mountain, they may resent and resist you. You get angry with them. In turn, they get angry with you. Instead of doing a motivational dance, you do a dance of death: You're the enemy, they're the slackers. A death-dance becomes a death-spiral.

by the audience to the audience

If the call to action is not a behavioral technique, not the close of a sale, and not an order, what is it?

Just as we do not know what happens to matter in a cosmic black hole, we can never know the psychological transformations manifested in the call. We can only know the results of that transformation: action. Since we cannot know what the call is by what happens inside it, we can only understand it by focusing on who delivers it.

Order leaders take control. Action leaders give up control. When the call takes place, control must be with the audience, not the speaker. And if the audience has control, it is the audience themselves that must deliver the call.

What is the call? The definition derives not in what is happening but in who makes it happen.

The call in action leadership *is the audience doing it.*

Since the motivator and the motivatee are the same person, the most powerful call to action is given by the audience to the audience.

DEVELOPING THE CALL

Since the audience, not the speaker, ultimately makes the call to action, develop your call by simply standing aside.

"My talent," said a coach of a famous college championship basketball team, whose motto was Forty Minutes of Hell, "is not to hamper them by coaching them."

A great Chinese horticulturist said, "The secret of my art is to refrain from trying to make plants grow. After planting them in the right way, don't touch them, don't think about them, don't go and look at them, but leave them alone to take care of themselves."

Giving control to others does not mean it's party-time, and we do business by forever wearing funny hats, tossing streamers and playing kazoos. Clearly, action leadership entails a certain playfulness and joy. (See Chapter 11.) But it also involves hard work, discipline and the ability to keep a firm grip on your operations. You do not want individuals subverting your overall plans by doing whatever they want. That kind of freedom is really slavery. Still, it is only through individual initiative that your organization can consistently succeed. A common misunderstanding about the call is that when you give control to others, you lose control. But just the opposite is true. If you don't give control to others, you ultimately are out of control. After all, controlling does not mean confining. Confining people limits their actions. Controlling people *directs* their actions. There are two aspects, then, of control: direction and action. Order leaders emphasize direction at the expense of action. By ordering people about, they impair their creativity and initiative. In squandering the people opportunity, order leaders truly lose control.

Furthermore, giving control to others means being in control of yourself, being patient, working hard, being skillful and disciplined. It requires mastering specific techniques as well as being open to character and spiritual growth. The techniques can be found in this book, the growth found in you.

three ways to win a war

The Chinese general Sun-tzu said that there are three ways to win a war. The best way is to win the war by not fighting it. The second best way is to win the war before you fight. And the least desirable way is to win by fighting that war.

The same holds true for the call to action. The best call to action is not to give it. Throughout history, people have been motivated to do extraordinary deeds when a great leader is but a memory in their hearts. The next best call to action is to give it without saying it explicitly, when you say in effect, "You know what to do; I don't have to tell you." The least desirable call to action is to come right out and say it. So we make the call happen — that is have the audience compel themselves to take the needed action — long before the call is made.

win the battle before the battle

Ancient Greek vases portray images of Spartan soldiers preparing for battle — not by getting weapons ready but by combing their long hair. Having undergone unspeakably rigorous training, they looked upon war as soft living. A professional football player on a consistently winning team said that his coach worked the team so hard in practice that when "he told us to go to hell, we looked forward to the trip." The Spartans and the football team won the battle before they went into battle.

So the call begins with you, and it begins long before you speak. It begins with your own training, answering the three questions on which all action leadership is based: What does the audience need? What do you deeply believe in? And what action do you want them to take? Review the techniques that help you answer those questions. Armed with those answers, you are ready to touch blowtorch to gunpowder. Here's how to make the explosion — the audience giving themselves a power call — happen.

"Stand aside!"

Decades ago, during Fordham University's football heydays, coach Jim Crowley delivered a classic action-leader's call. The call didn't come during his pregame oration. It came after the silence that followed the oration. Crowley turned to the student manager and said, "Open that door and step aside. Here comes my big Fordham team!" Here's what you do: Connect past, present and future — then stand aside and let your big team through that door!

Here's the way that you make that connection so the explosion happens.

THE PAST (THE DEFINING MOMENT) *MEETING THE FUTURE* (THE VISION) AT THE PRESENT (AUDIENCE NEED) *EQUALS POWERFUL ACTION.*

Or the call as an algebraic equation: DM x V x N = A^2 or DMVN = A^2.

"I'll be there for you."

Our executive's call to action to his sales force was simply this.

> *I'm here for you. So whenever you need me, I'll be there for you.*
>
> *After you leave this meeting, I want you to write me a letter. I want a minimum of three specific challenges on how I can help you improve your sales.*
>
> *I'm going to meet those challenges. I'm going to come through for you. That's my vow. That's your challenge. This is our promise to each other.*

The nominal call to action was his challenge to be challenged. But it was less a call than a triggering mechanism to set off the true call, which came from his audience. He gave them the freedom to choose. By making choices, *they* developed the call.

people power/fusion power

Like a fusion reaction, a powerful call to action is self-sustaining. A fusion reaction is the manifestation of Einstein's famous equation $E = mc^2$. It is matter becoming energy. When tremendous heat compresses hydrogen atoms so that they "fuse" and form a heavier element, helium, energy is released as light and heat. Once triggered, the fusion becomes its own triggering device and continues as long as hydrogen is available.

"We did it ourselves!"

So it is with the call to action. The triggering is done by the speaker firing a laser beam, as it were, of defining moment/need/vision into the audience's hearts. The speaker doesn't provide the call to action; the speaker triggers the audience giving themselves the call. When an order leader tells people to go to the mountain, it is a one-shot deal. However, when you take the time and trouble to do action leadership, when you have said and done things that resulted in people motivating themselves to go to the mountain, and when there, they can say, "We did it ourselves!", you and they have unleashed energy, creativity and good will that spreads far beyond the time, place and circumstances of that particular mountain.

a desperate need to trust

A few years ago, a new CEO of a large West Coast-based service company was to speak at his national manager's meeting. Since he was new to the firm, it was the first time most of the managers would see and hear him. He anticipated giving a presentation on the state of the business. But I persuaded him to give a *speech* instead. A presentation would communicate the facts, but facts weren't as important as his motivating them to believe in him and his leadership. I talked to his managers in the field and discovered that they did not need to know the state of the business. Of course, that was important information. But most of them knew generally what it was. He could inform in detail by distributing handouts. However, they had one compelling need. The previous CEO had made a number of arbitrary decisions without consulting management. The managers were angry with the leaders. During my interviews with them, they told me, "I just don't trust our top executives." Our conclusion: They needed first and foremost to trust the new CEO. We tied his speech to a single theme: trust. He talked about what he believed in and where he wanted to take the company. To do that, we fused the defining moment with the need and the vision. Here's how.

fallen star

His defining moment had come in a softball game several decades before. He had been a champion sprinter in high school but had broken his leg badly in a skiing accident and had never been able regain his previous form. A year after the accident, when playing a softball game, he hit a single to right field — and was thrown out at first base! "Until that moment, I had not let myself realize that I was washed up," he said. "But when I got thrown out, I knew like a ton of bricks falling on me that the person I thought I was — a track star — no longer existed. I knew that I had to find the new me." Being a star, he had disdained helping and being helped by other people; but once his star had fallen, he had to reach out beyond himself. "I realized I couldn't succeed without other people. I went from stardom to 'teamdom.' I realized that to rely on people, I had to trust people and they had to trust me." He was too new to the company to develop a vision for the business. He began developing a vision only after he had been there at least two quarters. But at that meeting, he challenged them with a vision of leadership, leadership based on trust.

By fusing the defining moment (thrown out at first) with the need (trust) and the vision (leadership shaped by trust) he gave a powerful, "off-the-cuff" speech (which he rehearsed more than 20 times) that was the beginning of a turnaround for the company.

ACTION TO TAKE:

The most powerful call to action comes not from the speaker to the audience but from the audience to the audience. To make that happen, understand that there are two parts to the call, the trigger and the call. You yourself control the trigger, which is getting the audience to take very specific action. The audience controls the call. How the call is converted to action is a mystery, just as it's a mystery how the electrochemical activities of 3 pounds of brain tissue became Beethoven's *Fifth Symphony.* Let the mystery be. Take great pains to know and shape what goes into the call. "Garbage-in-garbage out" is as true in the quality of action leadership as it is in the quality of manufacturing. But unlike manufacturing quality, which can be measured and shaped by statistical techniques, the quality of action leadership is not tied to numbers but emotion, experience and the mystery of the call. Its *results* can be measured in terms of net income, market share, etc., but if you try to measure and control people's motivation and the action they take, you are an order leader, not an action leader.

— Know that the call is a paradox. You want the audience to take specific action, but you must give them the freedom to do it their own way.

— Know the two parts to the call, the trigger and the call. When you pull the trigger, when you challenge them to take specific action, you shoot a laser into the critical mass of their need, setting off a chain reaction of audience-impelled action.

— To trigger the call, answer the basic questions of need, belief and action. Do not pull the trigger until you do answer.

— Make the triggering more powerful by integrating defining moment, need and vision.

— Fuse the audience's most compelling need with the call to action.

— Fuse the vision with the call to action.

— Fuse the defining moment with the call to action.

— Fuse defining moment, vision, need with the call to action.

11

Humor

ANYBODY NOT TAKING business seriously will have a flat line on the career monitor. But to take business seriously does not mean that we must be always serious about business. Business is not all serious. A great deal of it is ridiculous. If we are serious in ridiculous matters, we risk being ridiculous in serious matters. In a crazy world, being ridiculous and humorous can keep us sane. When we are in a box, laughter is sometimes the only way out. Humor, then, and a sense of humor are tools of leadership, as powerful as the defining moment.

fosters sharing

The dance is existential fusion. It is you becoming your audience and your audience becoming you. Paradoxically, in that fusion you both manifest your individuality. You can't get people to become both motivator and motivatee without transforming each other through the dance. Humor enriches that transformation. When we are amused together, we *fuse* together; when we laugh together, we come together, if only for a moment, and become one another and thus enlarge the possibilities that we will change, challenge and improve each other.

profound contempt

Just before the battle of Cannae in 216 B.C., Hannibal rode out with his staff in front of his army to reconnoiter the Roman formations. A Carthaginian staff member, named Gisco, expressed his despair over the size of the Roman army, some 80,000 troops assembled on the plain before them. Hannibal frowned and replied with mock seriousness, "There is one thing more astonishing, and you haven't noticed."

"What is it?" said Gisco.

"In all those great numbers of Romans," said Hannibal, "There is not one person named Gisco."

The staff burst out laughing at this unexpected jest, and riding back to their own lines, they repeated it to other soldiers. All who heard it laughed. The Romans, watching the staff and army laughing uproariously, concluded that the Carthaginians must be profoundly contemptuous of them.

Before the sun went down, the Carthaginians encircled and cut to pieces the Roman formations, inflicting one of the greatest defeats ever on the city. Hannibal's jest did not win the victory, but it may have tipped the scales ever so slightly in the Carthaginian favor.

avoids the too-serious syndrome

We often fail not for want of trying but for trying too hard, for being *too* serious. "No task," said Roman satirist Horace, "is too steep for humor." Constant seriousness grinds down our enthusiasm, depletes our energies and robs our repose. When we bear down too hard, we get brittle. And when we're brittle, we can break easily. Learning to relax and enjoy our situation helps us bounce back from failure and achieve a consistently high level of performance. He who laughs, lasts. Socrates was the bravest of soldiers and the wisest of Greeks, but he loved a good party, could drink libations with the best of the carousers and play games with children with gleeful abandon. Montaigne said, "I have been able to take part in public office without departing one nail's breadth from myself and to give myself to others without taking myself from myself. This fierceness and violence of desire hinders more than it serves the performance of what we undertake, fills us with impatience toward things that come out contrary or late, and with bitterness and suspicion toward people we deal with. We never conduct well the thing that possesses and conducts us. Most of our occupations are low comedy."

transforms audience's anger

Anger comes with the dance as surely as the sparks fly upward. The people you want to motivate will not always like you or like what you are doing or like what you want them to do or even what they motivate themselves to do. Clearly, you must be sensitive to why people are angry and attend to what's contributing to that anger, but often you can do nothing to prevent them from getting angry. Some people will be angry with you simply because you are in charge. Few people relish being the object of people's hostility. But too many leaders internalize that hostility and become angry themselves, and therefore less effective action leaders — even though the anger directed toward them may not be their fault or have anything to do with them as a person or leader. But if you speak with kindly humor, you can often turn a roadblock of anger into a roadway of cooperation.

transforms your anger

Humor cannot only defuse an audience's anger, but it can defuse your anger as well. The adage "Engage brain gears before operating mouth" applies especially to action leadership. It has been said that the difference between a successful and unsuccessful career is leaving five or six things unsaid. A high-level client of mine has what he calls the "black box" solution to his quick temper. Whenever he gets angry with someone, he doesn't speak but writes a vilifying letter instead. "I make it smoke. But I don't send it. Don't send those kinds of letters. I put it in my black box (a cardboard box painted black) so it never sees the light of day. Then every couple of years, I sit down alone, have a scotch, open up the box and read what I'm glad I didn't send." What is said cannot be unsaid, but what is *not* said can be said any time.

With humor, you don't have to have a black-box solution. If, in your anger, you can see and communicate the humor in the situation, you need not write the letter. You need not leave a thing unsaid. Humor can reduce or eliminate anger or even make it work for you.

wins disputes

Humor is often proof against apparent logic. During the 1984 presidential campaign, the Democrats believed that they had a logical issue: Ronald Reagan's advanced age. At 73, the Democrats argued, Reagan was too old to perform well for four more years in one of the world's most demanding jobs. The voters, the argument went, should elect the younger Walter Mondale. The issue became one of the most prominent in the campaign — until Reagan and Mondale debated. Standing beside Mondale before a national television audience, Reagan said with great conviction: "I've told my staff that I will not let my opponent's youth and inexperience be an issue in this campaign!"

The gibe was a defining moment in the campaign. Not only did people across the country laugh but Mondale himself laughed too. The television camera showed Reagan expressing the line, then Mondale guffawing. He had to laugh. The line was funny.

If he hadn't laughed, he would have looked like a sourpuss. But in laughing, Mondale lost the issue. Laughing with Reagan, Mondale was laughing *at* the issue. Afterward, Reagan's age did not play an important role in the campaign.

reveals personal self

Humor is the mirror of the soul. What we laugh at, we are. Often, when humorous, we communicate more than we intend about ourselves. But as action leaders, we can use humor to communicate things about ourselves that we normally wouldn't communicate seriously. For years, the great comedian Jack Benny's trademark was his cacophonous sawing on a violin. Audiences laughed at his ineptitude. Yet his humor came from anguish: Benny was truly very good — though not good enough to be what he had so desperately wanted to be, a concert violinist. If he had wrung his hands and cried about his failure, his revelation would have been mundane, the world being full of frustrated violinists. But making that revelation humorous, he made it momentous and memorable. Since revelation gives meaning, necessary risk, and intensity to the dance, we multiply and intensify our revelatory experiences through the prism of humor.

reveals the audience to themselves

Humor is a communication switchblade; it makes people both see and *feel* the point. As with the defining moment, so with humor: You can reveal yourself to the audience *and* reveal the audience to themselves. Often, an audience is more likely to accept criticism if there is humor in that criticism. Furthermore, they are inclined to understand new insights about themselves if they can laugh about themselves or their circumstances. Be careful: A fine line exists between laughter and anger, just as your audience can laugh at your humor so they can, by feeling its point, get resentful too.

communicates emotion

We dance to emotion in action leadership. When you speak from the heart, you speak to the heart of your dance partners. But let's use emotion wisely and well. As we formulate our thoughts, let's formulate our feelings. The dance is not a Dionysian rite of emotional frenzy. Don't get your audience drinking from a fire hose of emotion. Using humor is a way of skillfully communicating emotion.

ACTION LEADERSHIP HUMOR

First, avoid canned jokes. To share, we must trust in the other person's integrity and ability. We must be genuine, not disingenuous. Though telling canned jokes does not make us untrustworthy or disingenuous, still, it contains an element of artificiality, often even insensitivity.

The structure of the canned joke, build-up/punch-line, is eternal and too often tiresome. Most canned jokes that I hear are *not* funny. I laugh to avoid being embarrassed by not laughing.

make pain funny

Clearly, there are wonderful hilarious jokes, jokes that often point to new insights. For when a thing is funny it usually holds an inner truth. By making us laugh, jokes make us more human and thus more ourselves. "I became a true comedian," said Roseanne Arnold, echoing the concept behind Jack Benny's violin *schtick*, "When I learned to take the pain in my life and make it funny." The jokes that cropped up among the people of the

Eastern Communist bloc during its final turbulent years (e.g., "They pretend to pay us and we pretend to work,") are masterpieces of humor and wisdom.

But generally, the canned joke, precooked, prechewed, predigested for spoon-feeding, is not as effective as genuine, spontaneous humor.

humor is not ridicule

We would rather do business with people we like, not with people we don't like. This doesn't mean that we can substitute likableness for results. The old joke about one salesman saying, "I had a great day! I made a lot of friends for the company," and the other salesman replying, "I didn't make any sales either," is an age-old business truth: We are not in business to make friends but profits. In business, people like us for who we are but, more importantly, for what we can do for them — though, in most cases, we can do more for each other when we like each other.

If likableness is the lubricant, though not the drive shaft, of action leadership, then making fun of people thins that lubricant. If the pie is in the other guy's face, it's funny; if it's in your face, it's not funny. If you are making fun of somebody, you're not likable. If fun must be made, make fun of yourself. Let people laugh with you by laughing at you. To dance well, get rid of the twin prejudices that enslave us: the prejudice for ourselves, i.e., self-conceit, and the prejudice against others, i.e., sex, race, or ethnicity. Cultivate the divine art of self-deprecation.

to the East

To get an example of the kind of humor we may develop in action leadership, let's have Montaigne point toward the East. Montaigne said, "Constant cheerfulness is the surest sign of wisdom." In the East, joy and wisdom are practically the same thing. The name of one of China's greatest sages, Lao-tzu, means in a broad sense, "the joyful old fellow." Laughter, wit and joyfulness were essential characteristics of many of China's sages for thousands of years. They weren't grinning idiots. They recognized that life can be brutal and tragic. Many sages lived in violent times and, to protect themselves, became masters of martial arts. But they taught, as do the Hindu Upanishads, the Bible, the Koran and the treatises of many other religions, that the way to the enlightened life is through joy. Most of us are familiar with the Chinese statue of a laughing fat man dressed in rags. Many mistakenly call it the "Laughing Buddha." He is not Buddha but Potai, an enlightened sage who wandered the cities and countryside in China, a great humorist, a great teacher of wisdom as well as a great favorite and playmate of children.

humor is wisdom and leadership

Potai and other sages instruct us in action leadership. After all, they were great teachers and, because people flocked to them and took action from their wisdom, great leaders as well. The sages' humor and cheerfulness were important components of their magnetism. As action leaders, we need not become wandering, homeless sages to attract people to our cause. But let's recognize that humor, kindly humor that flows spontaneously from the moment, has a measure of wisdom in it and is, ultimately, leadership in action.

take and work your bloomin' guns

Action leadership entails more than simply being knowledgeable about finance, marketing, sales, production and other functions of your business. Clearly, you must know your business, its products, processes and systems. And, to paraphrase writer Rudyard Kipling who said, "To win your battles, take and work your bloomin' guns!" you must also work those bloomin' functions. A Thoreau, a Potai or a Montaigne couldn't run your business, no matter how wise and heroic their efforts. Churchill said, "Wars are won by professional armies, not heroic militias." Business success is achieved by professionals staying close to their business day in and day out, not by dilettantes. Yet we in the West too often believe that knowing marketing, finance, etc., are both necessary and sufficient. Clearly, they are necessary but within the context of action leadership they are far from sufficient.

candles and arc lights

Action leadership requires more than a capacity for what is traditionally seen as functional; it also requires a capacity for the spiritual. The requisite marketing, finance, sales, etc., vital though they are, are dim candles compared to the arc lights of wisdom, courage, compassion, and, yes, humor. The culture of the order leader has customarily celebrated function not spirit. But if action leaders do not celebrate and commit to both, they will be like the Visigoths who called themselves Romans because they put on togas but were not Romans but only Visigoths in togas.

you can and must use humor

Unlike the often arcane disciplines of business, which take years to master, the spiritual side of action leadership is every day, every moment, within our command. The spiritual must be functional. As an action leader, you do not have to meditate on a mountaintop. Your mountaintop is your business. Your meditation is the dance. Every day you lead, you have the power to manifest courage, compassion, wisdom and humor. Humor is not a gift. It is something we all have, even though some of us may not recognize it. If it were a gift, it would come from outside us, be given to only a few people, and have little to do with our will. The importance of courage, compassion, wisdom and humor is that they are dependent on our will. They do not fall upon us but spring from us. We are free to manifest them or not. Action leaders not only can manifest humor, we *must* manifest humor. Humor is too powerful a leadership tool to let rust.

a texture of joy

Laughter has little to do with humor in action leadership. Humor is more a sense of joy than laughter. The word *humor* comes from a Latin root word meaning "moist and fluid." Humor should be fluid. It is not simply point-to-point joke cracking. It should flow. The goal of leadership isn't to get people to laugh but to obtain results. If laughter contributes to their getting results, so be it. But in most cases, your humor is to help create a texture of joy in the dance. Creating that texture is not easy and it doesn't happen quickly. But if you follow these techniques and apply them daily, you will begin to see an agreeable transformation in yourself and the people you lead.

HUMOR IS A SKILL

Humor is not a mystery of muses but a practical skill. You can develop it with patience and diligence, as you develop any skill such as repairing motors or cobbling shoes. After all, the sages I mention did not come easily to their wisdom, spontaneity and joy. They underwent years of rigorous meditation to reach their enlightened states. But to think they attained something is a mistake too. Their personalities simply *flowed.* You can't know them and their lessons as one might study chloroformed butterflies pinned to boards. The glow of their temperaments was in the flow, their wisdom in their words and actions. Humor in action leadership is a process not a point.

HUMOR BEGINS WITH YOU

We see things not as they are but as we are. So humor begins with us. We have an imagination for what we aren't — and humor for what we are and have been. I'm not just talking about going back in our past and dredging up humorous incidents to spice communication. That is a good technique, and it should be used. You won't be the first leader to remember funny incidents in your life; write them down and communicate them many times in many ways. But there is an even more valuable technique. Actually, it is more than a technique. It is a principle by which to act.

the Great Scowl

Boxer George Foreman provides the example. Foreman fought his way out of the projects of Houston, Texas, to win the Olympic heavyweight championship and then the world heavyweight championship in the 1970s. Foreman had a *schtick*: the Great Scowl. He went about in public, his mouth a straight line, his eyes burning under his brows with a mixture of anger and contempt. Before a fight, Foreman would fix his opponents in the Scowl's crosshairs, causing many of them to give up before the first round bell rang. Then Foreman got knocked out by Muhammad Ali, defeated by another opponent and then retired, somewhat broken in spirit. But then came the transformation.

the Great Scowl gone

Foreman underwent a religious conversion. He became a preacher. He returned to the ring more than a decade after he retired. But Foreman's making a comeback in his late 30s and early

40s, overweight, his skills rusted but with most of his punching power intact, was not the amazing thing. The amazing thing was that the Great Scowl was gone, the glowering predator Foreman was replaced by a humorous, compassionate Foreman, a truly funny Foreman. He said, "I made up my mind that when I came back to boxing and got back on TV and in front of all the media that I wouldn't take it seriously, that I would have fun. Too many of us take life too seriously. Of course, I had to be serious about my training to avoid getting badly hurt, but I wouldn't take all the rest of it seriously."

an American Potai

Big-bellied, loose-muscled George Foreman became a kind of American Potai. At the end of a slugfest with an unexpectedly tough opponent, exhausted though victorious, he grabbed the microphone in the ring and said to the crowd, "Anybody have aspirin?" Once when he was fighting, he turned and shouted comically at his corner, "Will you stop telling me what to do; he might be listening!" Turning back to the opponent he got hit flush on the jaw and, though hurt, mugged comically to the ringside fans. After the same fight, being interviewed on national television, he held his swollen face and said, "Where's my Momma? Oh, Momma, I hurt!'"

Whereas the scowling George Foreman had been feared and respected, the new, humorous Foreman became a beloved sports figure. Ironically, in his youth, when he took fighting so very seriously, people stopped taking him seriously when the aura of invincibility was shattered. But in his transformation, when he decided not to take the hoopla around fighting seriously, people then took him more seriously than ever by taking him to their hearts.

action without self assertion

George Foreman's comeback teaches that if we can step back from a troubling situation, not take it as seriously as it might seem to be and then bring a touch of humor to it, we may prompt action without self-assertion and development without domination. Humor is always with us and in us and ready to be used by us and can be called upon to change reality.

THREE PRINCIPLES

1. *recognize*

The skill of humor is based in fully conscious recognition. Don't get lost in your wandering thoughts and feelings. Cultivate the ability to give yourself wholeheartedly to a task and also to keep fully mindful of that task. Whatever you do, there should be a part of you watching and recognizing. If, as Montaigne says, we never conduct well that which possesses us, then to conduct things well, we must possess them — not in a grasping sense but by a sense of recognition. Being aware of things, we re-know or *re-cognize* them and thus make them ours, ours not to hoard but to give. For we do not truly possess a thing until we give it away. By constantly recognizing what we are doing and what others are doing *when we are doing it,* we are building a strong base for developing the skill of humor — humor not like a sudden cloudburst, coming and going, wetting quickly but not thoroughly, but like a steady, misty drizzle that soaks clear through.

2. *empathize*

Though humor is within us, it is for our audience. It is always for our audience, never for us. It is a forgetting of ourselves for them. *In the midst of our recognition of the moment, we reach out and see the humor for them.* It is Foreman reaching beyond his exhaustion and pain, grabbing the ring mike and asking for aspirin. It is Muhammad Ali in the throes of Parkinson's disease mugging for the cameras. It is Reagan on the operating table, close to death after being shot, saying to the doctors, "I hope you're not Democrats." It is my father calling my mother, him and me the "Cancer Crusaders" with that wise-ass salesman's wink as he once more got painfully into his car to be taken for yet another operation shortly before he died. It is Abraham Lincoln getting shot at by distant Confederate sharpshooters while inspecting Union positions and answering the young officer (Oliver Wendell Holmes Jr.) who shouted, "Get down you fool!" by saying with a grin, "I'm glad to see that you know how to talk to a civilian."

we are what we think

Clearly, humor didn't change Foreman's swollen face, Ali's Parkinson's disease, Reagan's wounds, my father's cancer and Lincoln's being shot at. It didn't change objective reality. But humor changed people's *perception* of the person undergoing that ordeal and so the ordeal itself. Just as product quality is what customers *think* it is, so reality is often what we think it is. We think and act most powerfully when we forget ourselves and emphathize with others. Humor is a form of courage. In his fear and agony, my father was able to laugh at his cancer, and when we who were with him laughed too, the cancer's power over all of us was diminished. We could not change the fact that the cancer was going to kill him, but in laughing, we were drawn closer together and empathized in ways we had never done before, and so achieved a kind of healing that transformed our relationships.

3. actualize

How do you bring humor to life's conditions? One way is to recognize that life's conditions are, in many cases, humorous, no matter how apparently depressing they may seem. For joy may be in the most insufferable circumstances.

There is a story that comes from the East of a man being chased by a tiger. The man tumbles off a cliff and grabs a sapling to keep from falling hundreds of feet. The thin sapling begins to crack. Hanging between the tiger's jaws and the death drop, he sees a wild strawberry growing beside the sapling. He picks the strawberry and puts it in his mouth. *How wonderful it tasted!*

death camp experiences

That story resonates in the experiences of many people living in the most bestial circumstances. Michajlo Mihajlov in his article "Mystical Experiences of the Labor Camps," an analysis of the writings of authors who were imprisoned in Soviet labor camps, observes that their incarceration formed the most "profound and significant experiences in their lives... Although they underwent the most extreme spiritual and physical suffering during their imprisonment, they also experienced a fulfilling happiness undreamed of by people outside the prison walls. . . . Deep in the human soul is an unfamiliar force which is stronger than all the external forces of enslavement and death."[1] And Jacques Lusseyran, who blind and helpless, was thrown into a Nazi death camp, wrote that the key to his survival was living in the moment. "We had to live in the present; each moment had to be absorbed for all that was in it to satisfy the hunger for life . . . . Don't hoard. Eat the food right away, greedily, mouthful after mouthful, as if each crumb were all the food in the world. When a ray of sunshine comes, open

---

1 Mihajlo Mihajlov, "Mystical Experiences of the Labor Camps," in *Kontinent 2*, ed. Vladimir Maximov et al., Anchor Press/Doubleday, Garden City, N.Y., 1977.

out, absorb it to the depths of your being. Never think that an hour later you will be cold again. Just enjoy."[2]

humor is often serious

Like Michelangelo's statue imprisoned in stone, humor and joy can be found where we are and in what we do. Our role is to free that humor, just as Michelangelo freed the statue. Comedian Victor Borge made an enormously successful career out of one thing: He found humor in the formal concert environment and freed that humor. We free humor for our audience's sake. It sounds easy, Michelangelo made sculpting sound easy, Victor Borge's comedy seems effortless, but it is not easy. Being humorous is sometimes very serious business and must be cultivated through rigorous practice. Yet, paradoxically it often *is* easy, because joy and humor can spring from the moment. You can make the moment happen or let it happen — not by using canned jokes, silly limericks, practical jokes, not by going around with the comic equivalent of a lampshade on your head but by freeing the humor and letting it flow through you to others. When your skill becomes refined, you will find that your humor comes with your hardly being aware of it, much like the moves of a great guard for the New York Knicks basketball team who said, "When I have the ball, my opponents don't know what I'm going to do next, because *I* don't know what I'm going to do next. I'm always surprising myself."

2 Jacques Lusseyran, *And There Was Light*, trans. Elizabeth R. Cameron, Parabola Books, New York, 1987.

ACTION TO TAKE:

Humor in action leadership comes from the living, breathing moment, that moment in which we act spontaneously. It is the same moment in which most athletes must perform, when they cannot consciously think and simply must act. After all, you cannot think but must instinctively act to hit a 90 mph fast ball, or slip a haymaker, or get out of the sprinter's blocks, or throw a shotput. But that instant action is made skillful by long training. To make your humor spontaneous, you too must train.
Here's your regime.

— Read funny books, not books on how to be funny.

— Watch funny movies. Listen to funny tapes. When you laugh, be aware of your laughter and why you are laughing.

— Study the humorous people in your life. Not the ones with put-down or joke-cracking humor but those with that humor that relaxes and makes people glad to be with them.

— Keep the company of children. Being themselves, they are continually illustrating how to live life. Let their joy enter you and flow out from you and into the people you deal with. Better yet, play with children, not as adult-to-child but as child-to-child. Many sages have been great playmates for children. A student of child psychologist Bruno Bettelheim said that his genius was that "when he spoke with a child, he *was not an adult but a child with that child. He put himself on an equal footing with the child.*" Picasso said, "I spent my lifetime on one quest: trying to draw like a child." When you can be a child with children, you can be a better leader of adults.

— Inject humor at the beginning, middle and end of meetings. Before the meetings begin, anticipate humor you might add and when you might add it. Ronald Reagan, as governor and president, always started off his first meeting of the day with a joke, either one he or a staff member related. Practically every day the staff had to come up with a good, new joke, more than 300 a year. Some commentators made fun of that and the fact that he read the comics every day. But Reagan started the day with a laugh and honed the skill.

— Inject humor into your impromptu remarks. I pretty much covered how to do that in my *Executive Speeches* book. In general, you can acquire a reservoir of quips, quotes and one-liners which you can thread into your communication.

— Write them in a notebook. I prefer the spiral-ring binder since the pages do not tend to rip as easily as ring notebook pages do. You need that non-rip quality since you should be referring to those pages a great deal. Watch for humor all around you, in your business, in the news, in your community. Later, when you have several notebooks filled, divide them into categories and cross index it.

— In a formal speech, be aware of the humor points, those points where "impromptu" humor is particularly effective: when you come to where you will talk, when you get up after being introduced and go to the podium; and after the speech is finished and before you sit down. A bit of humor at these points can be particularly effective.

— Inject humor into your defining moment.

— Get them laughing before the call to action. Often a call is made more powerful when given to an audience that has just laughed.

— Finally, let yourself, frequently, have a good, hearty laugh, especially when others are trying to be humorous.

12

Delivery

WHEN I FIRST started developing the concepts for this book, I gave low priority to speech delivery techniques. After all, I thought, when speaking from the heart, what need have we of technique? Delivery isn't what you do on the outside but what you feel and communicate from the inside. What does it matter how we stand, move, act and enunciate? Isn't the heart's passion enough? When people feel deeply, don't they speak eloquently? But today I have come up in the world; I've changed my mind. Having taught the principles and techniques of action leadership to many leaders, I realize that people do indeed need help to deliver action-leadership speech.

SET FREE

To understand why, let's go back once again to old foundations of new ideas, and look at the root word of delivery. It comes from a Latin root meaning to set free, *de-liberate.* When we "deliver" in action leadership, we are liberating something. What's confined? It's emotion. Emotion needs to be freed, to be delivered. Furthermore, it is *you,* the leader who needs deliverance. As we saw in Chapter 3, emotion by itself is a dysfunctional tableau. We must know why the emotion is being felt. If emotion defines the speaker, that speaker has a communication problem. An angry man is only an angry man. The speaker instead should define the emotion. A woman angry over an injustice is a woman on a mission. Structure and stories help shape those definitions. But so does delivery. The following are eight principles and 15 techniques of delivery.

1. TEAR DOWN THE PODIUM

Leadership starts at the place where the leader speaks. Because the position of order leadership speech is elevation, whether physical, psychological, social, or political, order leaders make a podium out of the place. They must remain on a high level to make themselves and the order more impressive and powerful. But a podium hinders action leaders, who must dance on the same level as the audience. During the last stages of the Soviet empire when statues of Communist leaders were being toppled, the manager of a statue factory said, "This young generation is thinking that statues are made to be torn down." Likewise with podiums for action leaders. Keep tearing them down.

first sergeant action leader

The Marine Corps is the last place one might think of looking for action leaders, but some of the best action leaders I have come upon have been Marines. A first sergeant I know has unique ways of tearing down podiums. He is 6-foot, 2-inches and has a big neck, big jaw, broad shoulders, huge hands and a pushed-in bridge of a nose. If your mission is to get on the other side of a wall, he would get you there but might not look for a door. The troops love him. As one of the sergeants under his command said, "He always sticks up for his men. He always tells people exactly how he feels. And he doesn't care who he tells, and he doesn't care how he tells them. And because he is outstanding in his job, they've never been able to hold him back for very long."

don't forget the troops

His guiding principle is, *accomplish your mission first, but once that mission is accomplished, take care of the troops.* That principle echoes an ancient Chinese general who said that the key to leadership was "in times of great difficulties, never forget the troops." The first sergeant has lent money he could not afford to lend to down-and-out troops, has frequently chewed out officers who were "messing with my troops" ("I go through a lot of hassles trying to straighten out young officers") and has put his career on the line in a number of ways by placing others' interests before his own.

"The troops can talk to me informally if they want," he says. "A lot of people feel that if they don't put out a certain image, their troops will try to take advantage of them. I know my troops will try to do that to me sometimes. And I just yell at them or do whatever to get them to stop. And I've always had confidence in my ability to do it. I've never been unable to do it, so I don't worry about it. If I ever get to the point where I can't do it, then I guess I'll have to project an image like, 'I'm up here, and you're down there.' My men should be like me, and I should be like them. You have to have compassion to be a leader. You can't just tell people to do something, and that's it. Sure, there are times when you give orders. But there are times you have to motivate people to figure out their own solutions. Most will get a solution if you don't get in their way."

4 feet, 11 inches

Action leaders come in many guises, not only 6-foot, 220-pound Marines but, as in the case of a CEO I talked about in *Executive Speeches*, a 4-foot, 11-inch, 100-pound business leader. Too short for lecterns, she gets off the podium and out into the audience to deliver her remarks. Leaving her notes behind, she asks questions about their needs and thus has the audience participate in the development of her speech. The Marine and the CEO demonstrate that action leaders must always be looking for opportunities to be like the people we lead and have them be like us. Both teach that getting off the podium, whatever that podium may be, is a highly personal as well as powerful art.

2. BE AN UNDERDOG

Shortly after *Executive Speeches* was published I received a call from the vice president of communications of a large corporation. He said that he had read the book and liked it and was in town, and would we have lunch together? During lunch, he had a habit of starting to speak but then stopping himself, as if he wanted to tell me something important but didn't know how to go about doing it. Finally, at dessert, he leaned forward, looked earnestly into my eyes and said, "Bland."

"What?" I said, confused.

"Bland," he said.

I said nothing. It was reminiscent of that moment in the movie *The Graduate* when an executive draws the young Dustin Hoffman aside at his graduation party and says in a low, important voice, "Plastics!" — a single word that is supposed to encapsulate broad, rich territory.

"Speeches," *this* executive went on, "must be bland." He said that boredom in corporate speeches wasn't to be condemned but commended, that executives must absolutely not stick their heads up at the turkey shoot of speech events. The first rule of corporate leadership, he asserted, is *never take chances, especially in speeches.* As he talked, a spot of color came out on his cheek. *He was getting passionate about being bland!*

the power of bland

We miss his point if we merely laugh it off. His point is that in a relentlessly order-giving culture, bland is often best. Being a prod, an order needs to be a sharp point. The push behind the point is a function of power, not compassion and human relationship. Power is often most effective when wearing an expressionless face.

But action leadership is not sharp-stick power. It is not "thrustmanship" but relationship. It is not being a top dog but the underdog.

the power of the underdog

The dance is not entertainment. It must get results. It is meant not to make friends but to make your numbers. And the spirit of the dance, of action-leadership speech, is the fighting spirit of the underdog. To motivate people to take action, be viewed as wanting badly that action to take place. Bring an underdog attitude to the relationship and foster an underdog attitude in your partners even if you are a top dog. I'm convinced that you cannot give truly motivational speeches unless you have failed bitterly in life. Most great achievements began in rejection. Being an underdog is a treasure; never exchange it for the complacent life. But as an underdog, don't be high-strung and excitable. The fiercest effort is not incompatible with an ability to relax. Try hard cheerfully and with humor. Having fun as an underdog is the art of delivery in action leadership.

3. BE HONEST

Delivery in action leadership is honesty in action. We discussed honesty in Chapter 7. But there is always more to learn about it, for honesty is a house with many mansions. You don't have to know it intellectually but live it devoutly, and in living it, be constantly learning new things from it and about it.

Long ago, in China, a general's messenger came upon a woman crying outside her front door. He asked what was wrong. She said that she had just learned that the general had saved her son. "My son had an infected leg, and your general saved his life by sucking out the infection."

"But your son is saved," the messenger said. "Why are you weeping?"

"He's not saved," she said. "He's healthy now, but he's lost to me. You see, the general saved my husband's life too. My husband lay wounded in snow. The general came upon him and gave him his only cloak and saved him from freezing. Exposed to the cold, the general himself almost froze to death. My husband was so taken by the general's actions that he fought without taking a backward step in the next battle and was killed. I know my son will be enamored of the general too now, and he too is going to fight like my husband and be killed as well."

a lesson in delivery

Looked at within the context of human relations, the general's actions bespeak compassion. But viewed within the context of leadership, the general provides a lesson in delivery, a lesson in the communication of honesty. Since people cannot dance effectively unless they know their partner is being honest with them, what better communication of honesty could have been accomplished by the general than risking himself to save his soldiers?

In the infantry, the most effective leaders I knew did not get out of the cold until their troops were warm, did not eat until their troops were fed and did not take shelter until their troops were under cover.

Do the many acts of service for the people you lead and you are practicing sublime delivery techniques.

service and comfort

Don't misunderstand action-leader service. It's different from customer service. In most cases, you are not challenging your customers to work hard. You are making life easier for them by helping them solve problems. But as an action leader, you must be constantly motivating the people you lead to learn more, do more and be more. Action leadership isn't about comfort and convenience. You serve "your" people not to make them comfortable but to better enable them to make the customer comfortable. Making the customer comfortable often involves our being *uncomfortable.*

the spirit of Garibaldi

When you are comfortable in business, you don't get inspiration but are headed for expiration. Being comfortable is like being wrapped in the coils of a python. That a python crushes you is a myth. In truth, a python is a clean, gentle creature that *embraces* you almost lovingly. With your every exhalation, a python takes up a little more slack so that you can't inhale quite as fully as before. Eventually, you can't inhale at all and you expire.

Leadership is a spiritual journey. If the journey is too easy and comfortable, its spiritual meaning is lost. Don't bring comfort to the people you lead. Serve them not by making life easy but interesting, by giving them responsibility and thus bringing them trouble and challenge. As the Italian patriot and general Giuseppe Garibaldi said in his call to action, "I offer neither pay nor quarters nor provisions. I offer hunger, thirst, forced marches, battles and death. Let him who loves his country with his heart, not with his lips, follow me." You're not offering forced marches, hunger, and death to the people you lead, but you can challenge them to be motivated by the spirit of Garibaldi and his poorly equipped, outnumbered but high-spirited and triumphant army.

4. LET ANGER BE

Action leadership isn't all sweetness and light. It doesn't anesthetize you against life. It is not a dance in *Brigadoon.* You must dance to the tune being played on the dance floor you are given. It recognizes as the Laotian proverb does that "When the water is high, the fish eat the ants, and when the water is low, the ants eat the fish." As you must know what you see, so you must know what you feel. Bring all the emotions to the dance. Say what you feel and feel what you say. Let speech harmonize with action. If action leadership is transparent leadership, then your feelings should be transparent as well. But here is the objective: Be aware of your feelings as you feel them. Don't lose yourself in them. Don't try to control them. Just be aware of them. That is especially true of anger. Anger can be a powerful tool of action leadership. Often people cannot motivate themselves unless they are disturbed. Anger gets things stirred up like few emotions. You don't have to study delivery techniques to communicate anger. Be angry, be aware you're angry and techniques (See ACTION TO TAKE) will come naturally.

be angry yet caring

A few years ago, a 55-year-old man was hired to be CEO of a family-owned manufacturing business. The firm's founder had just retired and the CEO was hired to run the company until the founder's son, a recent college graduate, could take over. The CEO was an unlikely looking leader. Stocky, bald, baggy-eyed and an indifferent dresser, he stuttered and was somewhat shy. He had a gentle, unassuming manner.

There was a fly in the ointment at the business: The founder's son. An only child, he was arrogant, rude and lazy. But the father, wanting him to eventually run the firm, had put up with his behavior. For years, the employees had cajoled and appeased the young man. But the new CEO didn't. His third day on the job, he dropped his gentle manner, had an angry confrontation with him and fired him outright.

There followed weeks of turbulence, the son trying to get reinstated, the father prevailing on the CEO to rehire him, employees not knowing one day to the next if the CEO would quit or be fired himself.

implicit injunctions

Yet during those weeks, the CEO was taken into the hearts of the employees. He had started in the industry as a teen-ager on a production line, had never gone to college, but knew the industry, production, marketing and quality control cold. But that's not all: If he found a washroom in the plant dirty, he would not order somebody to clean it but would take a bucket of water, a mop and toilet brush and do the job himself. (His initiatives became powerful injunctions to keep the washrooms and every other space in the plant particularly clean.) If there was trouble on a line, he would often leave his office and pitch in to rectify it. He and his wife were known to take gifts to workers when they or their family members fell ill. He even helped with the housework in the homes of the ill people. Often he could be seen cheerfully helping unload unexpected shipments of parts. As it turned out, the CEO made the firing stick. The firm went on to great success, no small part due to the CEO's inspiring leadership.

5. BE ADEPT AT *AIKIDO*

Developing an emotional relationship in action leadership entails trust and self-sacrifice. Some people warp that relationship through distrust and selfishness. They get you stuck to the tar baby of their egotistic self indulgence. They demand more of your time and emotions and refuse to let go. You may develop a relationship based not on business proficiency but on psychological deficiency, while others who are more deserving of your time and commitment are neglected. Finally, you may have to fire those difficult people for their good and the good of the business. That final choice must always be available to an action leader. You must know it — and your partner must know it. But there are many choices, short of firing, that can be made when leading those people. The key to dealing with difficult people before a decision to fire them must be faced lies in delivery, the delivery found in *aikido.*

integrating breath and action

Aikido is a Japanese art of self defense that uses grips on the joints, such as wrists and elbows, to immobilize or throw opponents. But it is much more than throws and pins. Derived from three words, *ai* to integrate, *ki* breath control, and *do* way, aikido is based on the concept that when attacked by somebody, your true opponent is not the attacker but yourself. Conquer yourself and you cannot be conquered. We must understand *conquer* not in terms of overcoming but in terms of realization and being. Conquering ourselves in aikido involves integrating our breath with our actions. It is a way of looking at reality and actualizing reality. We concentrate on ourselves and forget the opponent. Ultimately, as we advance in aikido, we forget ourselves and our opponents and simply dance. As the founder of aikido said, "The training is to take God's love, which produces, protects and cultivates all things in nature, and assimilate and utilize it in our own body and mind."

a hair upon an ocean

Our relationships with difficult people are usually based on a repetition of psychological and behavioral patterns. When we don't like somebody, we show our dislike and get disliked in return. It's a sniping relationship fought out on a single line. Eventually, that line becomes all in the relationship and consumes all. Yet, in truth, that line is as significant to our being as a single hair upon an ocean. We make the hair, not the ocean, the object of our passions and thus lose not for want of trying but for want of understanding.

Aikido recognizes that though the attack is always linear, the response must be holistic. So in dealing with difficult people, with being attacked through words, actions or even inaction, we find the response always within ourselves. When we change ourselves, we change the attack and the attacker.

"Man's greatness," said Albert Camus, "lies in the decision to be stronger than his condition. And if the condition is unjust, he has only one way of overcoming it — to be just himself."

A salesman friend of mine said it another way, "Love the people that hate you. It makes them madder than hell!"

the message is the messenger

The culture of attack-politics provides an example of how these concepts apply in leadership and communication. Conventional wisdom in U.S. politics asserts that when attacked, attack right back; hit them harder than you get hit. But in counterattacking, you are merely creating another line. You are focusing on the hair, not the ocean. Candidates who base their campaigns on communicating only the issues are particularly vulnerable to attack politics. But communicating the issues is only part of a candidate's communication challenges. As we have seen in this book, the truly important communication is of your individual essence. Most candidates either don't know this or can't do it. In action leadership, the message is not just the message; *the message is the messenger.* Action-leader candidates are not immune from being attacked but are usually not harmed seriously by those attacks. In fact, they are often helped since the attack boomerangs against the attackers. After all, the attackers are going after not a cardboard cutout dressed up as a white paper or a set of issues but someone with communicated human dimension. When a person you know and love is attacked, you can't stand idly by. You get into the fray too. That's why action leaders, when attacked, seldom lack people willing to take up their cause.

an exercise in self-definition

When you know who you are, live who you are and communicate who you are, for your sake and your audience's sake, then working with difficult people and dealing with their attacks becomes an exercise in self-definition. Freedom comes from definition. When seeing others' faults, let's look for and change those same faults in ourselves. "When somebody convicts me falsely," says Montaigne, "I don't learn some new thing he has told me. That would be a small gain. Instead, I learn my weakness in general, and the treachery of my own understanding. . . . I learn to mistrust my gait and always strive to regulate it." The best way to demonstrate that a stick is crooked is to lay a straight stick beside it. Being trustworthy and compassionate is the surest way to remind others, even our critics and naysayers, to be the same.

ignore, forgive and forget

Don't fault the crooked stick. If you're fault-finding, you are not engaging in action leadership aikido but in sniping. When hitting back, you are fighting on a line rather than manifesting your many dimensions. Don't quash difficult people or have others quash them in your name or the name of your cause, but instead dance with them as you would dance with others who are easier to work with. I understand that the CEO at the family-owned manufacturing firm never said a derogatory word against the son, even after the young man was fired and was rebuking him to employees every chance he got. Great delivery also involves ignoring, forgiving and forgetting.

beneficial difficulties

There is practical advantage in trying to work things out with people who are being difficult. Since you are creating opportunities of change and growth, you often find that difficulties turn out to be blessings.

Years after he was fired by the CEO, the son returned to work at the firm, a transformed man. He told me, "Getting fired was the best promotion I ever got. He taught me that if I wanted to do well in this world that I first have to do well by people. If I ever head this business, I want to be like him."

6. BE A CHINESE BASEBALL PLAYER

Action leaders must be able to play Chinese baseball. Chinese baseball has the same rules and equipment as American baseball except for one difference: When the pitcher releases the ball, any player can move the bases anywhere as long as the ball is in the air. Business today is Chinese baseball, a game of ambiguity. Leaders who can't live with and thrive on ambiguity, who can't adapt to their business game being constantly changed, will fall by the wayside. Since order leadership was built on and given direction through order, it requires that change be gradual and relatively predictable. But such leadership has difficulty coping with sudden, unpredictable change. By giving freedom not orders, by having power with people not over people, action leadership doesn't simply deal with change, it *is* change itself. Here are two principles to help you play Chinese baseball.

—let it!

Action leaders must know when to lead and when to follow in the dance. Whereas the style and substance of order leadership is attack, action leaders must know the art of retreat as well as attack. In many ways, surrender and gentleness are the most powerful motivators of all. You can often master a force by simply letting it be.

A short time ago, I gave a seminar on leadership communication to a group of senior executives on the West Coast. One of the participants was a successful owner of a service company. A jet pilot in Korea, he had been shot down and spent months in a North Korean prisoner-of-war camp. It was a particularly inhuman camp, with ramshackle huts ripped by brutal Mongolian winds, with medical supplies so scarce that prisoners cleaned their wounds with the only somewhat sterile liquid they had, their urine.

Yet having undergone that searing experience, he wasn't hardened and bitter, as one might expect, but good humored and resilient. He possessed a wonderful laugh. After the seminar, we were driving to a restaurant and the car broke down. We started walking toward a distant gas station. It had been drizzling while we drove, but as soon as we got out, it began to pour. Within minutes, we were soaked. "It never rains in Southern California!" I said bitterly, quoting the song. His thin hair plastered against his head in the rain, he looked at me sideways and winked and grinned.

Then he said two words that I won't forget. "Let it," he said and gave that laugh of his.

acceptance is freedom

Suddenly, I had a minor defining moment. I had an inkling of the strength that had helped him survive the camp, strength that was born in the philosophy: *Whatever comes, the good, the bad, the ugly — let it.* Surrender to it — not by being defeated but by accepting it. Because acceptance allows us to respond resiliently to change, such acceptance is not fatalism but freedom.

The pitcher winds up and pitches — the bases get flung all over the field — let them!

shock and understanding

Our acceptance doesn't inoculate us from upset and shock. Sure, change can be shocking. Nobel Prize-winning atomic physicist Niels Bohr said of quantum mechanics, the theory that subatomic particles act not with precision and purpose, as scientists for centuries had believed, but instead with the randomness of corn popping in hot oil, "Anybody who is not shocked by quantum theory has not understood it!" Often change hurts, angers, shocks, dismays and frightens, but in the boil of change find a measure of calm in knowing that it is an end and a new beginning.

two maracas

Actor Jack Lemmon tells of preparing for a key scene in the movie *Some Like It Hot.* He struggled for days rehearsing. Showing up on the set to do the scene, he knew exactly how to play it. But then he found himself in a game of Chinese baseball. Director William Wilder changed the rules. He handed Lemmon two maracas. "Play the scene with these maracas," Wilder said.

Lemmon was devastated. Playing the scene with maracas wasn't in his plans. All his rehearsing was down the drain. He tried to beg off, but Wilder insisted.

So Lemmon shook off the shock and threw himself heart and soul into the scene. It turned out to be one of the funniest in a very funny movie.

combat advice

Lemmon's experience echoes the advice of a Catholic priest I met on a training exercise in a Philippine jungle. He was German and had been an officer under Erwin Rommel in the North African desert. Captured by the British and imprisoned in Texas, he entered the priesthood after the war and became a missionary in the Philippines. At night, he would materialize out of the jungle, wearing a light cotton shirt, peasant's pants and sandals, and talk with me in a tent under a hissing Coleman lantern about his great passion, military tactics. "Always remember, Brent," he said, "*no plan* survives first contact with the enemy." He could play Chinese baseball too.

Because we do not know how change will turn out, let it. For change has many masks and its present fearsome countenance may hide another face. "Prosperity is not without fears and distastes," said Francis Bacon, English essayist, philosopher and scientist, speaking of the uses of change, "and adversity is not without comforts and hopes."

the worst emotion of an order leader

A key reason that change is confounding to order leaders is that it is often humiliating. Back in my own order-leader days in the infantry, I happened to be in Pickle Meadows, Calif., a very cold place, in snow with my platoon on skis. They were lined up in formation. I was skiing past them, got my ski tips crossed and fell over on my face. Right in front of them. They laughed. The bastards! I thought. How humiliating! I got up and stupidly, ridiculously, furiously chewed them out. I should've chewed myself out instead! I should have laughed with them. Where was my sense of humor? It was lost in my order-leader sense of pomp and circumstance. I had just encountered sudden change, had just fallen off my "podium" flat on my kisser and was feeling the order leader's worst emotion: humiliation.

bear humiliation

A secret of leadership is that great leaders are able to bear humiliation and bear it gracefully and if possible humorously. For humiliation is often caused by our realizing that we have shrunk to our normal dimensions. The Japanese, who are masters at institutionalizing deep psychological needs, understand this secret and have incorporated it into their corporate culture. They engage in "change-hats" activities in which workers get away from the work place with their bosses, drink, play light-hearted games and have intimate conversations. The purpose is to relax and to bring the bosses down to earth. Often during those occasions, bosses are chided by their tipsy workers. What is said and done during "change-hats" is left there. Grudges are not held. Rebukes are forgotten.

high-tech manufacturing rooted in soil

The psychological need that "change-hats" answers is the grounding of leaders. People can accept their leaders being on a podium but only to a certain extent and for a certain length of time. All leaders must occasionally come down off their high place if only briefly. The Catholic Church recognizes this, and the pope once a year washes and kisses the feet of poor people. The Marine Corps recognizes it too and organizes chow lines with lowest ranks eating first, higher ranks eating last. The last person to get his food in the mess is the commanding officer. That's a change-hats kind of ceremony.

Organizations that do not ground their leaders through ceremony, symbol or in actuality, such as change-hats, run the risk of angering their people. Humans, not demigods, lead people; but when leaders take on the trappings of demigods (today manifested not by miracles but by parking, travel, dining, housing and pension perks), they inspire displeasure instead of devotion.

Because the Japanese have integrated their ancient rice-producing culture into modern high-precision manufacturing (rather than eradicate that culture, as had been done to Western agricultural cultures in the Industrial Revolution), they have a more ceremonial sense than we Western businesspeople that all people, leaders included, come from the soil and must periodically return to and be grounded in that soil. Change-hats then is a ceremony of the soil.

smoke from other chimneys

The Japanese have developed a leadership culture because they covet social intimacy, but the Americans so far have avoided developing such a culture, because we covet social mobility. About as close as we have come to providing change-hat ceremonies are the traditional office Christmas party or an ocasional staff picnic. Our mobility is a root cause of this deficiency.

island harmony

Historically, in North America, if you didn't like where you lived or whom you worked for, you could pick up and move. Daniel Boone said that whenever he saw the smoke of another chimney, he moved on and built another cabin where no such smoke could be seen. Businesses are islands. People who work in them have to get along like island people by establishing a culture of group harmony. Being an island people, the Japanese are masters at establishing such a culture in business. If Americans are to regain mastery in business, we must have leadership predicated on island-group dynamics. That means we must recognize the need for leader-grounding. There are no new frontiers to flee to. The answers must be found in here-and-now relationships.

rigidly order-leader culture

Japanese change-hat occasions usually take place away from the work site. Japanese work culture, despite its focus on consensus and participatory management, is a rigidly order-leader culture. Japanese executives must clearly understand who is above them and beneath them. In most cases, they cannot function as equal partners in an enterprise. This hierarchy may not be discernible from the outside, but it is powerful and pervasive in practically every Japanese business. So the Japanese have institutionalized getting their order leaders off the podium, but because their leaders are essentially order leaders, they must be taken off the podium only when they are away from the work site. Otherwise, they need to be elevated on the site in many subtle ways not apparent to outsiders.

the humble can't be humiliated

Action leaders, not needing a podium, have no place to be knocked down from. They can be easily and naturally humiliated on the job. But the humiliation they might bear is not truly humiliation. When you become your audience and your audience becomes you, changes taking place that may mortify an action leader — such as falling flat on your face in front of the troops — are nothing more than opportunities to express joy in the dance.

—use it!

Let it! is not enough. You must accept change and use it as well. Plutarch said that Hannibal's great failing was that he could achieve a victory but not use it. Action leaders cannot be creatures of change; we must make change our creatures. "Freedom," said Jean Paul Sartre, "is what you do with what happens to you." It can be argued that the most important American founding father was not Washington, Jefferson or Adams but James Madison. The co-author of the *Federalist Papers* and called "Father of the Constitution," Madison almost single-handedly made the great changes of the American Revolution work by helping create one of the most enduring and elastic forms of government in history. Without his systematizing and bringing checks and balances to change, the Revolution might have gone the way George Bernard Shaw said most revolutions go — not lightening the burden of tyranny but "only shifting it to another shoulder."

don't get mad, get involved

When you find yourself playing Chinese baseball, don't get mad, get involved. Become a great Chinese ballplayer. Master change by putting it to work for you. Have fun doing it. And because you are not a complete action leader until you impart action-leadership skills in the people you dance with, be a mentor, be a teacher and be a coach. That's delivery that will live in the hearts and the actions of others for decades to come.

7. CONNECT WITH THE MASTER

Every person we encounter is our master in some way. There is no one to whom we cannot apprentice in some area of knowledge, experience or spiritual development. No matter how exalted in status we may appear to be, we must, as action leaders, find and connect with the master in the person we dance with, even if we dislike (or *especially* if we dislike) that person. When we do, we can make a deeply genuine and human bond that transcends superficial delivery techniques.

8. BE SILENT

The speech is not an intellectual expression calling for an edifice of propositions and proofs but an emotional *impression* that can be communicated by as brief a thing as a sentence, such as when an Olympic basketball coach waited in silence until just before the gold-medal game was to begin and said to his team, "You were born to play in this game!" Or the speech can be communicated by a single word, such as when Marine Corps legend and much decorated Lewis B. "Chesty" Puller rose before 5,000 retired Marines in a California ballroom in the early 1960s, men who had fought with him in several wars, and said one word which brought down the house with a long, emotional, standing ovation: "Marines!"

speeches without words

Speeches can be reduced not only to a sentence or word but also to silence. If the best way to win a war, as the ancient Chinese general Sun-tzu said, is not to fight it, then sometimes the best way to win a speech is not to speak it. When you have nothing to say, don't speak. Too many business leaders say the wrong thing at the wrong time simply because they spoke when there was nothing to speak about. The distinguished British actor, John Gielgud, was asked at 87 what was the single most important lesson he learned in his career. He replied, "To keep my mouth closed. I talk too much!" As Lincoln said, "I shall never be old enough to speak without embarrassment when I have nothing to talk about." Even when you have something to say, you can often say more by saying nothing. Delivery without words can be the most powerful delivery of all. As pianist Artur Schnabel said, "The notes I handle better than many pianists, but the pauses between the notes — that's the art!"

forms of silence

Silent speeches come in many forms. When the Chinese general gave his only heavy cloak to the wounded soldier in the snow, he gave a speech without words.

When the CEO of a major corporation recently walked into a room where his top executives were assembled, saw that his chair was isolated at the head of the group, picked up the chair and placed it in the middle of their group, he gave a speech without words.

Know that by engaging in those silent acts of service, honesty, trust, and commitment you are giving powerful motivational speeches.

8. PROVIDE CEREMONIES AND SYMBOLS

One of the ways I misspent my youth was hitchhiking around the nation, picking up odd jobs here and there and then moving on. I met an American Indian who was hiking along a highway, carrying a backpack. He said he was on a vision quest, walking and camping across the United States to seek a vision to enrich his life. I asked what changes he saw. He replied, "Nothing's changed, because I have my daily ceremonies."

Ceremonies and symbols are codified ideas and impulses and thus powerful delivery tools for action leadership. Ceremonies are formal acts or observances that help bind people to an idea, cause or goal. Symbols are material objects that stand for those things.

The former involves action and experience, the latter condensed philosophy. Both provide strong triggers for motivation. Like the American Indian whose daily ceremonies drew a centering plumb line through his quest, action leaders can center their activities in the hearts of their dance partners through the skillful use of ceremonies and symbols.

great motivational tools

We have all participated in ceremonies and been touched by symbols. Religious and military organizations make particularly effective use of ceremonies and symbols in motivating people to take action. The most effective leaders I have worked with around the world have used the tools to great effect. They have encouraged traditional ceremonies and made up their own as well as their own symbols.

ACTION TO TAKE:

Liberate, communicate, and deliver the individual you to your audience.

— Get off the podium and walk out among the audience to deliver a talk. Of course, you will be leaving your notes behind. But you do not need to refer to notes if your speech is not a monologue but a dialogue with the audience. Have the audience participate in the development of your speech.

— Ditto for the informal talks you give across a desk or a conference table or just standing face-to-face. Do away with barriers between you and your audience. When sitting at a desk, make "clearing-the-decks" movements to show you are removing work to speak. Get close to your audience and face them. Practice persuading with your ears. Keep focused on your audience; don't be distracted by ringing telephones and movements around you.

— Communicate honesty by doing the many little services that can help your audience. Critics say that high-paid leaders are wasting time and money by doing scut work. Clearly, you can't become your plant's janitor. You must carefully pick your times to do that sort of work. But do it. It will have enormous payoffs in binding your audiences to you and will serve as a strong motivational trigger.

— Don't suppress your anger, use it. Know that the remedy to anger is delay but that also there are times when your anger can be a powerful tool of motivation. But before you speak from anger, do three things: Tell the audience you are angry, tell them why you are angry then say one thing appreciative about them. Praise does wonders for people's sense of hearing.

In that way, you allow *them* to be aware of your anger. Your *honest* appreciation helps disconnect *their* anger. Pour your spirit into their humanness. Speak through your anger not to their anger but to their hearts.

— Don't part in anger. It is no failing to feel anger and show it when engaged in a heated discussion. The great failing is for you and the other person to go away angry with each other. Anger is like a breeder reactor that keeps producing more psychological contaminants than can be consumed. Before you part, shut the reactor down. Shake the other person's hand, look him in the eye and say in effect: "We have our differences. We got angry. We may get angry with each other again. That's OK. But let's leave our anger here and not take it with us. Many more things unite us than divide us."

— Take a course in and read books on aikido.

— When you are caught unawares by others' anger or an attack upon you, use breath control. First get control of your thoughts not by trying to force them out of your mind or pin them down but by simply being aware of them. Let your anger exist in your awareness. Bring that anger down into a point in your body several inches below your navel. To Asian sages, this is a place of great power. In Japan, it is called your *hara.* Coordinate your anger with the in and out of your breathing. Think: *I am angry and breathing in. I am angry and breathing out.* As a Marine drill instructor once told me, "When I blow my stack with the recruits, I make sure that I do it by being calm inside."

— Be a bit of an actor or actress. IBM's Thomas J. Watson Jr. said that successful leaders have to "make a show of getting angry a lot more often than you lose your temper. You have to look more worried than you really are when trying to stimulate somebody to tackle a problem." This is not being deceitful. In good acting, as in good fiction, art is an invention that makes us realize the truth.

— Switch roles. Often, a leader's first instinct is to put difficult people into a box. But sometimes the best way to deal with them is to let them out of the box, give them freedom, responsibility and power. People accept risks better when *they,* not you, decide to take the risks. Give them tasks with true importance. Switch roles with them. I know a general who used to come up to young leaders in the field, pin his stars to the leaders' collar and the leaders' chevrons to his collar and say, "All right, you are the general, I'm the corporal. What do you do in this combat situation?" There are two ways you can do this: either through a face-to-face role play, or by actually giving the person a concrete task. For instance, if you face a hostile audience, say to one member, "Stand up. Be me. Now what would you say about the matter to this audience?"

— Stay humble. No matter how high you rise in your business, keep in mind that the perks you get, the red-carpet treatment you receive are only illusions of power and not power itself. "On the loftiest throne in the world," said Montaigne, "we still sit on our rumps." True action-leader power comes only when the motivator and the motivatee are the same person, when the people say, "We did it ourselves!"

— Be patient. A CEO of one of the largest companies in the United States told me, "I hate patience!" But remember that time is a powerful drug taken in small doses. Action leadership is for all seasons, not for a quarterly report. Like coral growing underwater, your becoming your audience and your audience becoming you should grow slowly and inexorably without being apparent on the surface of things.

— Be you. You best become the audience and they become you when you first become you. MGM mogul Louis B. Mayer said of Rita Hayworth's screen test, "She can't act. She can't talk. She's terrific!" You don't have to be Churchill or Joan of Arc. Be yourself, and you'll be terrific.

— Practice "pop-up" leadership. The most effective and charismatic leaders I have known all have a knack for "popping up," suddenly appearing, wherever they are least expected to be — at all hours of the day and night. "Never make a schedule," a Marine general told me. "If you do, never stick to it."

Engage in "pop-up" leadership not out of an attitude of spying but service, out of a genuine concern for helping them be more efficient, effective and productive. When people know you may suddenly appear beside them at any time, your presence is there even when you are not. Be careful. Use this technique judiciously. If you pop up too frequently, your lieutenants may think you are undermining their authority and the people with whom you interact may think that you are interfering in their work.

— Be aware of how change affects your dance partner. In your efforts to master Chinese baseball, don't forget that there will always be many people you work with who cannot abide the game. They will always have trouble with sudden, unpredictable change. Be sensitive to their anxieties and try to prepare them for the change before it happens.

— Be calm, or at least appear to be calm, when sudden, rapid change is taking place — even though you may not feel calm. The priest/military tactician I met in the Philippines told me of a time when he was given orders to lead troops in North Africa on a particularly dangerous patrol against the British. "It was practically a suicide mission," he told me, "But it had to be done. When I got those orders, I went out of sight and crapped. I couldn't hold my bowels I was so scared. I crapped and then threw up. When I was feeling a little better, I gathered the troops together and calmly told them of our mission."

Being calm is the wellspring of action. A CEO of a worldwide construction firm said, "You have to look like you have calm confidence in what you are doing. Even though you may not be 100 percent sure that you and your company can get the job done, you have to appear 100 percent sure. You have to exude an attitude of 'We can do it!' "

— Retreat to solitude. John Milton said, "Solitude is sometimes the best society and a short retirement urges sweet return." The Japanese tea ceremony is a refined art of making ceremony of solitude. The celebrants retreat to a simple hut usually on the edge of or in the woods and participate in an ancient rite of preparing, pouring and drinking tea. As with aikido, the meaning of the tea ceremony is linked to its outward forms and inward realizations. "Tea," said a Japanese general several hundred years ago, "is made with water drawn from the depths of the mind." As D.T. Suzuki said in his wonderful book, *Zen and Japanese Culture*, "Modern psychology gives us many cases of active businessmen, strong physically and mentally, who will suddenly collapse when they retire.

"Why? Because they have not learned to keep their energy in reserve; that is to say, they have never become aware of a plan to retreat while working. The Japanese fighting man in those old days of strife and unrest, when he was most strenuously engaged in the business of war, realized that he could not go on always with nerves at the highest pitch of vigilance and that he ought to have a way of escape sometime and somewhere. The tea must have given him exactly this. He retreated for awhile into a quiet corner of his Unconscious, symbolized by the tearoom no more than ten feet square. And when he came out of it, not only did he feel refreshed in mind and body, but very likely his memory was renewed of things of more permanent value than mere fighting."

As a Western leader, you may not have ready access to a Japanese tea ceremony as a retreat into solitude, but you can find and make your own ceremonies and so your own solitude. I love to lay up stone walls. For many years, I would leave my office for a lunch hour of stone laying. Mixing sand, mortar and water and building walls that were plumb and square with tight-fitting stone joints became a kind of tea ceremony ("Mortar is mixed with water drawn from the depths of the mind!") from which I always emerged refreshed. Do what you love to do. Climb cliffs, serve the homeless, paint landscapes, sail boats — find your true self by losing yourself in solitude. You need not be alone in solitude. The best solitude is often found when you have a companion or companions with you. When you return to the fray from a retreat into solitude, you'll find that your delivery is more natural and appropriate. Solitude, though, is a great place to visit but you wouldn't want to live there.

— Get people to help. *Your* best delivery happens when your audiences themselves are delivering. And they often best deliver when your call to action is a call for help.

13

The Global Action Leader

HUMAN RELATIONSHIPS GLUE business dealings in most cultures. But in North America that glue is thinner and less adhesive than elsewhere. The discovery of the New World caused a colossal shift not just in geographical relationships but human relationships. To a great extent, the immigrants to North America were not a heterogeneous people, from all walks of society, but homogenous, from the trades and working classes. In losing their relationships with their mother culture and entering a new world of opportunities, they formed a culture that placed less importance on human relationships in commerce and more on opportunity relationships. Because commerce opportunities abounded in the New World, we became a people who want to get down to business quickly. And like Mr. Scott (whom we shall shortly meet), in wanting to get down to business quickly, we have often missed the human opportunity in our hurry.

rediscovery

Advancements in communication technologies and transportation are changing the North American way of doing business. For as new technologies collapse time and distance, global speech opportunities, and the opportunities for intercultural leadership communication, expand. Because the principles and techniques of action leadership are grounded not in the order but in the relationship, they are well-suited for the international arena. Action leadership is about discovery, the discovery of and the reaching out to the hearts of our audience, and also about rediscovery, the rediscovery of what was sometimes lost in the winning of the New World: the Old World belief that we must simply get to know each other before we do business together.

A FABLE

To illustrate these ideas, let me tell you a fable. It deals with one Mr. Scott, a mousetrap and the Japanese. It happened that Mr. Scott had built the better mousetrap. Now he wanted the world to beat a path to his door. With mousetrap sales running off the chart in the United States, he was invited to Tokyo to introduce his product. He worked hard on his speech. This is what he said:

> *I've come here to tell you about an important new product, the Scott Mousetrap.*
>
> *The product is the result of a great effort in entrepreneurship. Individual initiative and creativity went into the design and manufacturing of the trap.*
>
> *With this mousetrap, we are going to help bring individual enterprise to Japan. I have hired one of the best salesmen of your country: Mr. Sato. He is sitting right there. Sato-san, please stand and be recognized. Believe me, he is a great salesman. He stands out above the rest!*
>
> *In the Scott company, we are all equal. We are going to go forward as equal partners and beat the competition into the*

ground! Our number-one goal is to make tremendous profits!"

resignation and devastation

The Tokyo businessmen politely applauded Mr. Scott's remarks. Scott was happy. He thought his speech was a great success. But no Japanese businessman came forward to help. What's more, Mr. Sato resigned.

Scott was devastated. Here he had built the better mousetrap, but he had lost his best salesman and his sales in Japan would never get off the ground. Unable to find Japanese partners, he flew home, wondering what he had done wrong.

salary men gone wild

The fact is that Scott had not done anything wrong. He had *said* it all wrong! He had failed to motivate his audience to take action because he failed to understand fundamental aspects of the Japanese culture.

In his speech, he extolled what he thought were great virtues of entrepreneurship, not knowing that for many Japanese such activities are censured. Entrepreneurs in Japan are called *datsusara* — salary men gone wild.

He had publicly praised his salesman, failing to recognize that public recognition is anathema to most Japanese.

Finally, he made possibly the greatest blunder by giving top priorities to profits, not knowing that the Japanese ideal emphasizes that profits are built on a foundation of social harmony and concern for human beings.

rewind the tape

Fortunately, this is an allegory in a high-tech age. Let's punch the rewind button. Let's go back to where Mr. Scott first began to prepare his remarks. When he was invited to give the speech, he should have asked himself a single question: What does the audience want or need to hear?

If Scott had acquainted himself with the Japanese culture, he would have known that his Japanese colleagues first needed to know about Scott himself. From his audience's perspective, their relationship was the first thing to be established. They wanted to know if they could understand and trust Scott. From that understanding, they would then have decided whether to do business with him.

shared values

With Scott now enlightened by a new understanding of the Japanese, he prepares another speech.

He begins by talking about the values he and the audience share, the first being a common commitment to the advancement of society through the development of a better mousetrap. He talks about the value of cooperation and describes a dramatic example in the development of his mousetrap, illustrating how worker cooperation shaped technological innovation. He then uses that incident to underscore that he and his audience have an opportunity to engage in a cooperative effort that will help further Japanese/American relations.

Having laid the groundwork of common values, he then describes his mousetrap within the context of those values.

the moral

The speech is a great success. Japanese business leaders tell Scott that they want to become better acquainted with him and his mousetrap. Mr. Sato becomes an important salesman for the company.

Simply by taking the trouble to understand his product from

the Japanese perspective, Scott has begun the process of successfully introducing that product in Japan.

The moral of the fable: People around the world can't be motivated to take action unless they get your point. To make sure they do, ask not what they can do for you but what you can do for them.

GLOBAL MEASUREMENTS

Today, with information circling the world faster than the time it takes to penetrate a human head, the power of nations doesn't grow out of the barrel of a gun but instead dances on the head of a silicon chip. With consumerism sweeping the world, today's Caesar might say, "I came. I saw. I shopped!" Like Mr. Scott, many of today's business caesars must be global leaders and so must thrive on the new orders of magnitude that global leadership requires. If your customers or potential customers are located around the world, you must view your market share globally. Failing to do so will be a boon to your competitors, since many of them will be viewing their share in world terms and taking actions to seize that share. If you don't make dust around the world, you'll eventually eat dust at home.

ACTION TO TAKE:

— Know the change. Technological advances are reshaping practically every society around the globe. Know the major changes that technology is making in the countries you will be in. List at least five of those changes. When you know what is changing in a culture, you have an idea of what people need.

— Know what is remaining the same. Changes in a culture always take place against an unchanging backdrop. When you understand that backdrop, you have an idea of a few of the motivational impulses of your audience. In many cases, that backdrop will be the values of the culture's religious, educational, political and social institutions. Too many global leaders do not study those institutions, especially the religious ones. They're neglecting an important opportunity. Even a cursory view of the religions can pay dividends in helping you understand people's needs and impulses. The people you lead do not have to be practicing the religion. Since they were raised in a culture configured by the religion, they are influenced by that religion in many conscious and unconscious ways.

— Know at least a dozen cultural taboos. For instance, the custom of shaking hands with other people differs from culture to culture. Know the handshaking rites, practices and taboos in the culture in which you are doing business.

— Know the convergence points. Where do you find your culture showing up in the society in which you will be leading people? Look for those convergent points in business, art, sports, entertainment, and politics. Study these points by asking what need is being expressed by the convergence. That need points to motivational triggers.

— Know the heroes and heroines of the society. Look for them and learn about them in the history of their military exploits, religions, politics, sports and industry. Study them by writing three defining characteristics of each person. Understand *their* defining moments. Those characteristics and moments indicate reasons why people in that culture are motivated to take action. They can also provide dramatic stories for your speeches.

— Read the introduction to as many of that society's cookbooks as you can lay your hands on. To discover a society's true needs, don't consult the wise men but the waiters. It is in what we eat, when we eat and how we eat that we often reveal who we are.

— Know the national holidays. Look beneath the surfaces of those holidays and ask what need they fulfill in their society. See the need in terms of emotion. What aspects of the holiday make people feel emotion? Each need is a window through which you can view the culture and from which you can develop powerful motivational speeches.

— Know the history of your industry in that society. When did it first begin? What was the need to have it begin? Who were the industry's founding fathers? Can they be made into heroes? Are there good stories to tell about them?

— Know the vision of the society. (See Chapter 9.)

— Know the benchmarks of individual success. In some societies success is measured by what you get. In other societies, success is measured by what you give. When you know the measure of success in society, you know that society's needs. Answer the question, "What are the attributes of a successful person?" and you have a call to action.

14

The Speech Begins after the Speech is Finished

THE SPEECH IS the cornerstone of action leadership. When you are motivating people to take action, plain speech is far more important than the written word. This book provides you with the principles and techniques for preparing and delivering the motivational speech. This chapter will help you make the speech continue to live after the words are spoken.

DEMOSTHENES FLEES

Demosthenes was one of the most persuasive of Greek orators. Single-handedly, without an army, wealth, or political base, using only the power of speech, he rallied the Greeks to go to war against Philip of Macedonia. But in the heat of hand-to-hand combat,

Demosthenes' acts did not match his words. Panicking, he threw away his sword and buckler and fled the field. The Macedonians triumphed and Demosthenes was disgraced. Years later, after Demosthenes' death, the Athenians erected his statue in brass, with the famous inscription,

> *Had you for Greece been strong as wise you were,*
> *The Macedonian would not have conquered her.*

As an action leader, be strong as well as wise, wise enough to give powerful motivational speeches but also strong enough to make motivation continue to happen after the speech is finished.

MOTIVATIONAL SPEECH IS A PROCESS

Don't view the speech as a discrete entity. Clearly, in its classic form, it is grounded in the audience's need, has a beginning, middle, and end, an explicit or implicit defining moment, a vision, and a call to action — all tied to the speaker's passionate belief. The motivational speech is a process — a process that, when action is taken, becomes prophecy. Its beginning is really the end of a previous event, and its end, the beginning of new events. When you finish your motivational speech and people begin taking the action you want, you have only just begun your motivational activities. Be wise and strong. Enhance the quality of the process and thus the quality of your leadership by continuing to apply the techniques. Here are ways to insure that you can continue to prepare and deliver motivational speech.

1. DEVELOP A MOTIVATIONAL CONVICTION

We know that the speech begins with the audience's need. But the process of continually giving motivational speeches begins with your conviction that whatever your audience is motivated to do, must and will get done, a conviction that you cultivate *and* communicate.

In Chapter 3, we talked of the "Not one man more, Westmoreland," conviction of Henry V before the battle of Agincourt. But Henry's conviction would have been useless if he had not transferred it to Westmoreland and the other troops. When his conviction became *their* conviction, his speech was given expression in their actions long after Henry's words were spoken.

he believed in me!

In the 1972 Olympic basketball finals, the Soviet team was ahead by 1 point with but seconds left. The Soviets were in-bounding the ball, but the United States' Doug Collins stole it and drove for a layup. A Soviet player dove into Collins' legs. Collins cartwheeled to the floor, momentarily knocked unconscious. As he got to his feet, an assistant coach shouted, "Get somebody else to shoot the fouls."

But head coach Hank Iba replied, "If Doug can walk, he'll shoot!"

Collins recalls that moment. "His words electrified me," he said. "*The coach believed in me!*" Motivated by Iba's conviction, Collins went to the line and took his shots. "I can't even remember feeling pressure," Collins said. "I hit 'em both and we got the lead."

The Soviets, however, won the game on a disputed call. But for Collins, his coach's belief was a defining moment in his life. He concluded, "I didn't know what I was made of until then."

conviction is not enough

Conviction reveals what you and your dance partner are made of. It doesn't come free and it doesn't come without effort. It must be constantly nourished with bold vision, new actions, and new commitments. And it must be underpinned by knowledge and training. You may have a conviction that you can run a four-minute mile, but unless you have the cardiovascular capacity and have undergone rigorous training, conviction alone will not make it happen. Communicate your conviction by insisting that your partners get the education and the training to master their tasks. This often means insisting that they become better than they are or at least better than they think they are.

exchanging paint

Action leadership helps people understand that they can be better than they are. I played junior high-school football in the Northeastern part of the United States. But at the beginning of my sophomore year, my family moved to the South. I had played relatively well in the North, and walking out onto the field for my first practice in the South, I was convinced I would be the team's star.

But I stepped into another dimension of football. Football in the North was *not* football in the South. Always our first workouts up North were light and easy. But suddenly this troglodyte coach had us running up a steep, red-clay hill. Up then down. Up then down. Then we started full contact! We went one-on-one in a sandy pit, exchanging helmet paint. Then it was more hill-drills. More head-knocking. While the summer heat, hotter than any I had ever experienced, made my eyeballs feel fried in their sockets. I threw up. I passed out momentarily. "Take a salt tablet and run it out!" barked the troglodyte when I came to.

Heatstroke pending, I bounced drunkenly from tackling dummies to the pit to the hill. After practice, I collapsed in the locker room, thankful that I had a day to recuperate, but through my ear-ringing exhaustion, I heard the coach growl that we had better hustle more in the afternoon. *The afternoon*? In the North, we had one practice a day. In the South, I found out, there were two — and sometimes three!

a lesson in challenge

Adversity reveals our true selves because we lose our admirers. That experience has taught me self-knowledge that I have brought to many leadership communication situations. Clearly, I'm not recommending that you go through summer football practice in the South to get a similar kind of lesson. (Coaches are much more knowledgeable about heatstroke today and the need to drink water, forbidden in our practices then, during intense physical exertion.)

But in experiencing what I alone would not have put myself through, what I had no idea that I could go through, I learned that challenging leadership must break the molds of how people view themselves. That coach, whose teams consistently won championships, made his conviction that we were better than we thought we were, our conviction too.

2. DEVELOP A MOTIVATIONAL ATMOSPHERE

I have been involved with losing and winning teams, losing and winning organizations, and, as I see it, the difference between losing and winning is atmosphere. Atmosphere is constant conviction in speech and action. Winners create an atmosphere in which success is always possible and losers struggle in an atmosphere in which success is seldom possible. Action leadership insists that the possible is always achievable and that the impossible just takes a little longer. It prompts people to say, through words or deeds, not "See what I can do" but "You ain't seen nothing yet!"

be there

The key to developing a motivational atmosphere is to be *there* with your audience. The president of a highly profitable raw-materials business attributes the secret of his success to the fact that "I am always there." Wherever his leadership is needed, he doesn't make an inordinate amount of phone calls, doesn't send memos, faxes or videotapes; instead, he sends himself, he shows up and speaks.

If you can't be there physically, be there mentally. Be constantly mindful of whom you want to motivate, their needs and the action you want them to take. Be ahead of them in terms of knowing what they will need to get things done. Be passionate about helping them solve their problems.

a master of supply

A battalion commander I knew was a master at obtaining the best equipment for his men. No battalion commander in the regiment trained troops harder nor gave them longer conditioning marches nor kept them in the field longer. Their morale was very high, partly because they knew that he was constantly angling to support them. The many stories that circulated of how he used his wits, displayed chutzpa and spent long hours working to help his troops were motivational defining moments.

In a desert exercise, when a logistical screwup hampered the distribution of water to the regiment, *his* battalion got the water they needed, though they were the farthest unit from the supply dumps. He had anticipated the water shortages well-before the exercise began and developed creative ways of supplying his men.

During the exercise, he raised hell with staff colonels who tried to confiscate his troops' water for their staffs and for a large party of VIPs. And when his troops got back to bivouac areas, ice-cold beer awaited them; the other battalions didn't get beer until they returned to the main base.

forget yourself

Creating and sustaining a motivational atmosphere entails not only your being there but, when there, forgetting yourself in the service of others. Before embarking on his Persian campaign, Alexander the Great gave his wealth to his commanders' families so they could live comfortably while the army was away. When asked what wealth he would leave himself, Alexander replied, "Hope."

When his victories brought great riches (before the affliction of absolute power transformed him into a tyrant who would, on a whim, raze towns and cities and put their populations to the sword), he gave those riches to friends, making them as wealthy as the wealthiest kings and causing his mother, in a letter, to admonish that in enriching his soldiers "you make yourself destitute." And when pursuing the defeated Persian king Darius across wasteland, he and his troops choked with thirst, Alexander gave a lesson in service. Offered a helmet full of cold water poured from skin bags by a party of Macedonians who were traveling from a far-off river, he had an opportunity to quench his raging thirst.

not a drop of water

Plutarch wrote, "Then he took the helmet into his hands, and looking round about, when he saw all those who were near him stretching their heads out and looking earnestly after the drink, he returned it again with thanks without tasting a drop of it. 'For,' said he, 'If I alone should drink, the rest will be out of heart.' The soldiers no sooner took notice of his temperance and magnanimity, than they cried out to him to lead them forward boldly, and began whipping their horses. With Alexander leading them, they said, they defied hunger, weariness and thirst and looked upon themselves to be almost immortal."

emulate success

Get help in helping others. Become a master at creating a motivational atmosphere by seeking out those who do it well and then do what they do. Gain success by copying success.

At his retirement party, a successful salesman gave a brief speech not about his achievements but about a single mistake he made early in his career: He neglected an opportunity to train with the best salesman in the company. "I was a green salesman assigned to help him cover his territory. But we couldn't get along, and I got a transfer. What a blunder! I was too inexperienced to see that the personality conflicts didn't matter! What mattered was having him educate me. If I had done that, I would have become a better salesman in a shorter period of time. The lesson for all salespeople, young and old: Find the best, stick to them, don't let them go until you learned all you can from them."

enjoy people

Leaders who don't enjoy people cannot create a motivational atmosphere. Without joy in the dance, work becomes a bore. Trying to motivate bored people is like trying to change tires on a moving car. If people bore you, it is your fault, not theirs. If you dislike somebody, look for the cause in you, not them. It is easier to change yourself than other people. But when you change yourself, the people you encounter often change too. When you communicate that you enjoy people, watch them change in wonderful ways.

monsters and villains

Just as you must find conviction in every motivational speech you give, so you must find those things that you enjoy in *every* person you want to motivate to take action. At the beginning of the lunch break at one of my seminars, a midlevel manager of a major computer firm said, "You say, '*enjoy!*' Well, I don't! My job and the people I work with are a big pain. I've been passed over, passed up, now I'm ready to pass right on out of the company. I'm in my mid-forties, and people ten years my junior are being promoted above me. Let's have lunch and I'll describe my work environment. Maybe you can figure out what's wrong."

No sooner had we finished the appetizers than I got a good idea what was wrong: His view of work was like a grade B sci-fi movie: he, the good guy, struggling to defeat evil aliens masquerading as humans. Most people he worked with were the aliens. Yet the very few people he liked were distorted in his mind's movie too, they being his gallant, heroic companions in the good-against-evil struggle. He wasn't getting ahead because "the aliens" were subverting him. It was a case of life imitating a shooting script.

people are what we think

"Powerful is the empire of habit," said a Roman philosopher. At lunch, I was not going to be able to help him break careerlong habits. I could only give the advice I give here: That people are often what we think they are. If we think of them as boring and stupid, they will somehow read our feelings and act badly toward us. But if we truly enjoy their company, most likely they will find joy in being with us. People are not cardboard cutouts, although we are often tempted to think of them and relate to them as such. All people are endowed with dimension, wonder and mystery. Action leaders must connect with those attributes.

the drama of the moment

There are a number of ways to make those connections. One way is to ask what prompted them to join the organization. Their reason for joining may be a defining moment for them. What was the drama of the moment? What changed them? What would they do differently if they had to go through that moment again? Nine times out of 10, you will have an interesting story that provides insights into what inspires and motivates them.

meditative listening

Another way to make that connection is by meditative listening and watching. "Listen to others," said a sage, "Even the dull and the ignorant; they too have their story." The best way to listen is simply to meditate. There are many ways to meditate. But as commonly practiced in most religions, meditation is simply a way of focusing the mind, weeding out scattered thoughts, with the goal of self-discovery. The focus can be on a word, a chant, a precious stone, a mantra — or whatever is taking place at the moment. The Bible says to accomplish with all your might the task that comes to hand. If that task be listening, do it with all your might. Which means listen meditatively. Make the focus be the people who are speaking to you. Weed out extraneous thoughts. Don't drive them away. Simply return your concentration to the people speaking and the words being spoken. Make the people, the words, the moment your mantra. Do it daily in every conversation. When you listen meditatively, you discover a lot more about yourself and about others than when you talk. People I know who listen in this way exude a special warmth that draws others to them.

meditative watching

As you hear, so should you see. Make meditative seeing a leadership attribute as well. Let people be by simply watching them. Watch with all your might. While watching, let thoughts, especially value judgments, come and go. Simply watch people as they are. Watch them as they do what they do. Do not watch them to change their behavior. Enjoy people by accepting them for what they are, not what you want them to be or do.

I find women leaders to be particularly adept at listening and watching. I asked a woman leader of a statewide social organization about this, and she agreed. "That's because women in our society are brought up to answer needs," she said. "Listening intently to people is a way of answering their needs." In answering needs, women are often more attuned to acknowledging and expressing their emotions than men are and more committed to leadership through relationship. For those reasons alone, women in the coming years will be many men's role models for action leadership.

transparent leadership

When I speak of listening and watching, I do not mean that leaders should be snooping. You listen and watch with people being fully aware of your being there. Action leadership is transparent leadership. Do not have hidden agendas, secret goals, favorite people, concealed observation sites. The democratization of information is an action-leadership imperative. Of course, few things ever happen exactly the way we plan. When we think that everything is perfectly clear to everyone, there is usually somebody who didn't get the message. And there are many times when people *shouldn't* get the message, or at least the whole message, such as when you are trying to develop a new product or program. But when in doubt, be transparent rather than secretive. If you cannot keep confidences, people will not give them to you.

criticize the action not the person

Many times what you hear and see will conflict with what needs to be done. The art of action leadership involves knowing when to get out of people's way and also when to get in their way and even get, on rare occasions, in their face. When you must reprimand and criticize, first express your appreciation for something that person did well. Communication doesn't happen unless the other person gets the point. People are more likely to get the point when they have an open mind. Sudden criticism tends to close and padlock minds. You cannot antagonize and motivate at the same time. After expressing appreciation, focus on the wrong *action,* not the person committing the action. There is all the difference in the world between saying, "I don't like what you did" and "I don't like *you.*" That is the difference between creating an atmosphere of enervation and one of motivation. Don't neglect the power of gentleness. As Plutarch said, "Those who have command of men should bring them around by the mildest and fairest of means, and not treat them worse than gardeners do those wild plants, which, with care and attention, lose gradually their wildness, and bear excellent fruit."

nightly assessment

Before retiring at night, reserve a few minutes alone to assess the opportunities you had during the day to create the motivational atmosphere. This practice was a secret of Demosthenes. We know that Demosthenes trained himself in oratory by speaking with pebbles in his mouth. But he did one thing more that is not as well-known. Every night, he retired to his study and analyzed the speeches given in the popular assembly that day. He rewrote those speeches to make them more effective. He analyzed the way people spoke to him in conversation and the reasons for their persuasiveness or lack thereof. He practiced giving speeches in front of a mirror. Demosthenes was not born an orator; he made himself into one.

get behind their eyes

Find time to retire and analyze. Become a fountainhead of ideas for the people you lead. Get behind their eyes. Ask if you are giving people all the help they need to do their jobs. Are you allowing them freedom to do those jobs the way they see fit? Rehearse brief speeches you may give them. Reorder those speeches to make them more effective. Do the people need to see you more? Do they need to see you less? (For often, your absence is a more powerful motivating factor than your presence.) How can you give more to them? How can you hustle for their sake? How can you find enjoyment in who they are and what they do? How can you get them to say, in one way or another, "You ain't seen nothing yet!"

virus of self-abnegation

In your commitment to serving those you lead, don't forget the other very important person in the dance: yourself. In avoiding the bacillus of self-centeredness, do not get infected by the virus of self-abnegation. Find time for yourself. Do what you like to do. "He who abandons healthy and gay living of his own to serve others thereby takes, to my taste, a bad and unnatural course," wrote Montaigne. When in a moderate way, you take care of *your* needs, your service to others is enriched.

3. DEVELOP A MOTIVATIONAL INCANDESCENCE

Action leaders should have an incandescence, a special glow of personality and character that draws the hearts of people to them. This incandescence has been called *charisma,* but charisma implies an almost-divine gift. Put the techniques of this book into action, patiently and consistently, like the elephant in the children's story who tries to hatch an egg by sitting very delicately upon it. You will find that you too are acquiring charisma, not a gift conferred but an inner glow, self-revealed. It is a matter of uncovering not igniting that glow; for you, as a human, possess it innately. That glow burns brightly when you forget yourself in the application of this book's techniques, but if you become conscious of yourself and the glow, it flickers and fades. Here are ways that you can make it light the dance.

use the defining moment

Like the motivational speech, the defining moment is not a point but a point of view, a state of mind and heart. It is a powerful technique for the formal speech. But it can also be used in the many informal speeches you, as a leader, give every day. Every speech opportunity *is* a defining moment, an opportunity to bring your past experiences and the past experiences of others to bear upon the need at hand. Since the defining moment is based on the premise that motivation happens when ideas become human and human beings become ideas, telling your audience of your defining moment is only one of many ways to use the technique to create an ongoing motivational atmosphere.

three principles

There are three principles to apply when continuously transforming things through defining moments. We've discussed the first principle: transforming you through your defining moment. Do not hide your light under a bushel. Defining moments are meaningless unless communicated. Make people aware of your defining moments, not for your sake but theirs, not to preen your ego but to serve them so they can transform themselves. We have all worked with many people who seem unlikable when we first met them but became likable when we got to know them. They didn't change. *We* changed. We got new information about them and saw them, and ourselves, in a new way. And when we see people in a new way, we often find that they begin acting toward us in new ways.

— transform a challenge into a defining moment

The second principle is to transform a challenge into a person's defining moment. Notre Dame football coach Knute Rockne applied this principle when he urged his team to "Win one for the Gipper!" The Gipper, George Gipp, was a small-town Michigan athlete who helped lead Rockne's 1919 and 1920 teams to undefeated seasons. Just before the 1920 season ended, he contracted pneumonia. On his deathbed, he told Rockne, "Rock, some day when things look real tough for Notre Dame, ask the boys to go out there and win one for the Gipper." Eight years later, before a mediocre Notre Dame squad took the field to play undefeated Army, Rockne told his team about Gipp's wish and said, "Now go out there and win it for The Gipper!" Inspired, Notre Dame defeated Army 12-6, halfback Jack Chevigny diving over the Army line for the winning score and yelling, "That one's for the Gipper!" The episode was made memorable in a movie with Pat O'Brien playing Rockne and Ronald Reagan playing Gipp.

Ostensibly, the Notre Dame-Army contest was a football game, but Rockne used a defining moment to make it a transforming experience for his players.

transformation technique

Make your challenge-to-defining-moment transformation this way: Say, "This isn't just an objective we must attain, this is (Describe a particular person and his or her defining moment.)"

— defining moment-to-challenge

The third principle is to transform a person's defining moment into a challenge. Nelson Mandela being imprisoned for decades in a South African jail was a case of the myth of the man being exceeded by the reality. Mandela was released because he had become more a threat to the government in jail than out. Make your defining-moment-to-challenge transformation this way: Say, "You aren't just you. You're much more than that. You are (Describe the challenge.)"

a treasure of defining moments

On your way to work, review the coming day. Think of the meetings you will attend, the people you will talk to, the challenges ahead and envision how you can use defining-moment techniques to best motivate people to take action.

In your day-to-day motivational efforts, you will seldom use your own defining moments, otherwise you may come across as the professor who said to the young student, "I've talked about me long enough. Now it's your turn to talk about me." But you have access to a treasure trove of defining moments that have nothing to do with you. You can find them in the people in your business, your family and friends, current events, your industry, history, sports, movies, plays — even in this book.

preparation

Preparation is the key. Before speaking the defining moment, anticipate, adapt, use.

Anticipate the situation in which you will use it. Be there before you get there. Anticipate how you might use a defining moment in a meeting, an informal talk, or a one-on-one discussion.

Adapt the moment to the situation. Describing an inappropriate moment, or a moment inappropriately, is dangerous. After all, the objective of the defining moment is to communicate emotion. If your audience believes that you are trying to manipulate *their* emotions, you are not going to motivate them.

Use the defining moment so that people are not conscious of the technique. Do that by making sure the defining moment exists for the fulfillment of the audience's needs, not yours.

the product disappears

Take a lesson in the art of concealment from the inventor of virtual-reality. With virtual-reality, people use body attachments rigged with computerized sensors and software models to experience the feeling of moving into artificial fields of reality. Using virtual-reality, one could experience the visual sensation of walking through a house that exists only as the manifestation of architecturally programmed software. The inventor of virtual-reality said that its success lies in the fact that when "the customer uses the product, the product disappears."

That is a key to the success of many products: At the moment that the products fulfill the customers' needs, those products disappear. The young man getting into a sports car doesn't get into just a transportation vehicle; he also gets into a compact cosmos of power, speed and sexual potency. The woman putting on expensive designer clothes is putting on not apparel but power. So it is with the defining moment; when it answers the audience's needs, it ceases to exist as a defining moment outside the audience. It becomes instead the hopes, dreams, commitments, actions and visions of that audience — transformations that often inspire an awareness of your incandescence.

"I goofed!"

Incandescence shines most brightly against dark tapestry. Your light cannot shine without the dance also involving misunderstandings and mistakes. Being human, you have a right to act stupid and make mistakes. Making mistakes shows that you are at least trying. Most of the time, the person who never makes mistakes will work for the person who does. But don't make a cult of mistake-making. Avoid them, of course — just don't view them with fear and trembling. And when you make them, admit them. The two most powerful words of leadership are: "I goofed!" Speak them. If your audience knows that you have made a mistake and you do not admit that mistake, they will mistrust you.

Employ the "I goofed" technique this way: Say it, rectify it, get on with it.

'no excuse, sir' attitude

Don't create alibis or excuses. A CEO who was educated in military schools says that the most valuable lesson he learned was to have a "No excuses, sir!" attitude. "People who make excuses for their mistakes don't learn from them," he said. "When you screw up, say, 'No excuse, sir!' — even if there are all kinds of excuses you might make. No matter how embarrassed you are by the mistake, taste and feel it to its fullest measure. Don't put on a hair shirt. You made a mistake, admit it. That's all. Only then can you truly be educated by it."

After you say, "I goofed!", rectify the mistake by saying exactly what you will do about your goof, how you are going to change things so that the mistake does not happen again.

Finally, get on with it. Put it behind you. Go on to other things.

acquire a signature

Most great leaders have acquired a signature: a gesture, an article of clothing, a phrase, a hobby, a talent, an enthusiasm — all a focal point for people's esteem and sometimes even ridicule. (For a leader is not leading well if he or she is not being ridiculed by some people. All great leaders in history were the object of ridicule.) Thus Montgomery had his beret; Churchill his cigar and two-fingered V sign; FDR his cigarette holder; Kennedy, his practice of *not* wearing a hat; Truman, his piano playing.

Leaders I know personally are recognized for sky diving, wearing no coats in the winter, wearing Irish walking hats wherever they went outdoors, and on and on. Choose a distinctive signature and stick with it through the years.

4. ALLAY THE FEAR-OF-FLYING

At the moment people decide to take action, a strange thing often happens. They may doubt themselves, doubt you, doubt the necessity for action, doubt the impulses to action. They undergo a kind of fear-of-flying syndrome and the personality change that goes with that fear: The calm become irritated; the congenial, hostile; the articulate, dumb; the happy, depressed.

This change is normal. People who are motivated to take action are stepping out of the known (which is comfortable, even though it may be, paradoxically, anguishing) and into that high-anxiety state: the unknown.

order leadership is a warm blanket

This fear arises in people associated more with action leadership than with order leadership. There is an element of security in responding to orders. To a large extent, recidivism is caused by prisoners leaving an orderly environment of regular meals and regulated activities and having to deal with choices in the outside world. "I found freedom *inside* prison with the authorities in charge," said an inmate I once interviewed as a journalist. "I could never cope with living outside where *I* was supposed to be in charge."

anxiety is free choice

Most of us are, to some degree, like the inmate. On one level, we do not want to be ordered about, few people do; but on another level, our responding to orders, in general, produces less anxiety than our having the free choice to act. So anxiety and personality change are natural to that moment when action is about to be taken. Expect them. Welcome them. When you understand them, use them to your advantage. Here's how:

watch the change

First, at the moment of action, look carefully for that change in your dance partners. An action leader must be a student of human psychology. Read people's weaknesses and strengths and play to them. Read what they are thinking by what they are doing and saying and even *not* saying. Look for tip-offs: a frown, a folding of their arms, an awkward smile, a shake of their heads, an avoidance of eye contact, or any number of things. Seeing the change, don't be upset. It is an inevitable reaction to a fear-of-flying.

allay their fears

Second, allay their fears. There are seven ways: 1. Build up their confidence. 2. Interject a greater fear. 3. Appeal to their courage. 4. Appeal to the team. 5. Keep and make eye contact. 6. Give an order. 7. Back off.

— build confidence

Build their confidence by restating the speech in a condensed form. Talk through your convictions to their needs and show them why the action must be taken.

Confidence comes from clarity. Be clear about the action. Make sure the audience absolutely understands it and the need for it. Hesitancy at the moment of action is often caused by the dance partners misunderstanding what really needs to happen. A goal clearly stated is a goal half-achieved. Boil what needs to be done down to one absolutely clear sentence. Get them nodding affirmatively, or have them repeat what you just said. You might say, "I want to make absolutely sure you understand this. Tell me what you heard me say."

switch roles

Another way to make sure things are clear to both of you is to switch roles. Say, "If you were me, what would you do in this situation?" Or, "I am going to be you. Being you, I'm going to talk about what should be done. Tell me if I'm right or wrong."

confidence builders

Once both parties are clear about the action then begin to build their confidence to take it. There are a number of ways to do this: Repeat what's at stake, talk about successful action they took in the past, about successful action other people have taken in those same circumstances, about the rewards of the action to be taken, or about the dire consequences of action not taken.

— inject a greater fear

Talking about the dire consequences is the second technique to allay their fears. It's fighting fire with fire. It's your mother saying when you were a child, "If you don't take this spoonful of castor oil, you won't grow." When your audience understands that their *not* taking action will lead to something worse happening, their immediate fear is often transformed into resolve.

Use this technique *infrequently*. As I explained in Chapter 2, fear is a powerful motivator but habit forming. If overused, it eventually becomes destructive to both partners. People who are consistently motivated by fear eventually become resentful and disinclined to be self-motivated.

— appeal to their courage

Action leadership should bring people together in courage, not divide them in fear. When people are reluctant to take action, an appeal to their courage often gets them moving.

An old salt of a Marine leader once said, "Of course, you've got to kick ass and take names a lot in the Marine Corps, but never, never tell them that they *aren't* Marines. Many of them are Marines because they are courageous. But many of them, also, are courageous because they are Marines. Don't tell them that they are not what they deeply believe they must be."

When appealing to your partner's courage, be subtle as a sock on the jaw. Tell them outright you believe in their courage. Be specific. Every person has displayed courage many times in their life. Tell them about those times. Let them know that you know. Tell them that the time is now to be once more what they have been on many occasions.

— appeal to the team

Deep in the engine room of human motivation lies the impulse toward community. Because humans have evolved as social animals, we have a powerful need to be part of a group. Appeal to the team to allay the fear of action. Often, if people think that their *inaction* will let down the team or remove them from the team, they are willing to act. You may say in one way or another, "The train's leaving the station. All aboard!"

— make eye contact

Eye contact is a more powerful motivational technique than many leaders realize. Often, you motivate people to do great things by simply looking into their eye and saying, "Let's do this!" Or even looking in their eye and saying nothing. I know a corporate leader who is a master at establishing eye contact for motivational purposes. She is very popular; her employees would walk on cut glass for her. At the moment when action is needed, I've seen her fix people with a steady gaze — and not utter a word. Her gaze says it all. I once asked her how she mastered this knack of seeming to communicate a lot without speaking. The question surprised her. Then after thinking awhile, she said, "You know what my secret is? I haven't thought about it until now. When I'm making eye contact, I make my mind a blank. In that way, they get the message because they give it to themselves. My gaze is really just a mirror that they look into. But it is a mirror into their soul."

— order them

Often, the only way to action is through the order. That seems to clash with the very promise and purpose of this book. But we are looking at that moment when motivated people become fearful and doubtful. Often, our plans cannot wait for people to motivate themselves to act. Action leadership is nothing if not practical. It is what it does. If we must wait for people to rev up, we often miss an opportunity. As we saw in Chapter 8, people sometimes need a push to action to be transformed by action.

— back off

Sometimes the best order is no order. When people are fearful to act, you may back off or even get away from them altogether. Some people need space, psychological and/or physical, to be motivated. If you crowd them, they become resentful and fearful. Some of the most effective leaders I know are not the grab-'em-by-the-throat-to-get-their-attention kind but are soft-spoken and seldom-spoken, with a proclivity for staying out of people's way. How many times has our desire to buy a product been made more urgent when we could not find a salesperson to take our money? Backing off can be powerful indeed.

the motivational pipe

Use the seven stops on the motivational pipe to play a variety of tunes. Action leadership entails having a passion for the music of people. Only when you know and are committed to people by enjoying people can you make the tunes and the dance get the results that you want. In that commitment and even in that enjoyment, you will, you must, experience difficulties. Jazz musician Miles Davis might as well have been speaking for the music of action leadership when he said, "To stay a great musician, you have to always be open to what is new, what's happening at the moment. You have to be able to absorb it if you want to communicate your music. Music isn't about standing still and being safe. I like playing with all kinds of musicians."

15

Beyond Motivation: Developing a Culture of Action Leadership

WE ARE NOT complete action leaders until we instill action-leadership concepts and commitments in the people we lead. That is most effectively done when we build a culture of action leadership in our organization. A Christian mystic said, "The eye with which God sees me is the eye with which I see God." So it is with creating a culture of action leadership: When people share a vision and values and ways to communicate them, they see each other with the same eye. That eye is the eye of culture. Developing that eye, building a culture of leadership, brings both dance partners into a common understanding of each other and of leadership. People who want to join that culture understand to some extent the challenges they must face in their participation. People who want to lead in that culture understand what is expected of them. And people being led in that culture understand the ways in which they can challenge their leaders to live up to the highest standards of the culture. Here are ways to build a culture of action leadership.

1. CULTURE IS QUALITY NOT QUANTITY

A culture is a state of quality, not quantity. You can develop a culture with three people as well as 3,000. For me, one of the best training grounds for action leadership was my being a playwright in New York City. I learned the craft of communicating emotion. While undergoing my playwright apprenticeship, I supported my family by working as an emergency room orderly on the graveyard shift of a Lower East Side hospital. There I learned, unexpectedly, about how a very small group of people can develop a culture of leadership.

action leader practical nurse

My boss was a great action leader, a 60-year-old practical nurse who had recently emigrated from Jamaica. I was one of three orderlies in his charge. He created a culture of leadership as powerful as any I have ever encountered. He demanded that we commit ourselves totally to serving the patients (he called it TPC, Total Patient Care, and TLC, Tender Loving Care), no matter who those patients were; and many were overdosed addicts or shot-up or beaten-up dealers who came from those mean streets. He had a broad, nut-brown face, framed by a full head of white hair, with deep crow's feet at the corners of eyes that could be fierce or kind at turns. I can see him now standing beside that emergency room entrance, through which would appear, in those wee hours of the morning, some awful manifestations of human anguish and destitution, his stethoscope looped round his thick, wrinkled neck, saying in that Jamaican lilt, "God's light! God's light! Everyone who comes here has God's light! So treat them right!" We orderlies loved him, though his demands on us were heavy and though we had many difficulties trying to meet his standards. When a new orderly joined us, he was expected to measure up to the standards or go elsewhere. Orderlies from other units of the hospital, admiring us, often tried to get transferred to our group. Truly, led by the nurse, we few were a band of brothers. So the first step in developing an action-leadership culture is to recognize that it is not magnitude but merit that defines culture.

2. CULTURE IS NEITHER ATMOSPHERE NOR TEAM

The next step is to recognize that a culture is not an atmosphere you create nor a team you build. Atmosphere is a distinctive quality of an organization or place. It shares attributes with a culture in that it is developed and maintained by a commitment to common values, vision and voice. A team is a group of people associated with joint goals and action. A culture can have a special atmosphere and is often composed of teams. But creating an atmosphere and a team or network of teams does not mean that you have created a culture.

the DNA of business

A key attribute of culture is that it is also a replicating mechanism. Culture is the DNA of an organization. Just as DNA contains an organism's genetic code, enabling it to replicate, so a culture of action leadership contains its own replicating-genes, its unique visions, principles and methods that can be transmitted from one generation of employees to another. Build a culture of action leadership for today and for tomorrow, and for tomorrow's tomorrow. Action without culture is only the actor's action, but action empowered by culture relates to all people in that culture, now and in the years ahead.

our culture was there

I discovered that our emergency room group had been more than just a team, that we had indeed created a culture, when I returned to visit the hospital several years after I had moved out of New York. The nurse wasn't there. He had taken a job in an upstate New York hospital. The two orderlies were not there either. Both had gone on to nursing school. But our team was there — not physically but *culturally.* For as I went down a hall to pay my respects to the chief physician of the emergency room (he had not left, though he had had nothing to do with creating the culture, all of that development being the nurse's), I happened to glance in a bathing room. There, sprawled on the floor beside the tub, wearing indescribably filthy clothes that crawled, actually seeming to move, with legions of lice, was a half-conscious old man, smelling like a brewery. His foot was swathed with a fresh bandage, and two orderlies were gently removing his clothes to give him a bath.

God's light

The sight made my heart jolt with a flood of memories. I had never seen those particular orderlies before. But looking at them, I knew them like brothers. Though the stink coming from the old man was like a pestilence and lice were on the orderlies' clothes and hands, they did not wear masks or gloves. Back then, years before the discovery of AIDS demanded that care-givers take extraordinary protective precautions, the nurse insisted that we never wear masks or gloves when attending to the patients, no matter how horrible a physical state those patients were in. "Serve patients with your spirit," he said many times, "Gloves and masks hide the spirit." Watching the orderlies serving the old man, I could hear the practical nurse's words, as if he were right beside me, "God's light! God's light! Treat them right!" These orderlies were giving the old man TPC and TLC. The nurse wasn't there, but on a deeper level he *was* there. His vision, values and voice lived in that emergency room.

That was when I realized that we had not created a team but a culture.

3. DEVELOP A HOLISTIC CULTURE

Your culture of leadership should affect people at their hiring and at their retiring and imbue all their activities inbetween. It must be the shape and dimension of water in which fish swim. Here are ways you can create it.

— *develop a vision*

Culture begins with your vision, is empowered through values and is communicated through your voice. To develop a new culture, to change an old culture, or to clarify and energize a present culture, reread the chapter on vision. Culture comes from the Latin word meaning *tilling* or a *place tilled.* You cannot till without a vision of what to till, plant and reap. Get the vision wrong, and the culture will be wrong. Get the vision right, and you are on the way to getting the culture right.

— *clarify values*

The "value statements" so many businesses develop have

become as much of a cliché in business as "motivation." Too many such statements are couched in the language of the intellect. Leaders make a common mistake of believing that the intellectual expression of values is the communication of them. The truth is, the language of values is the language of emotions. When you decide on the values to communicate, return to the techniques in this book, such as the defining moment, to make that communication take place.

— hire attitude

The richest area of resources in the world exists between people's ears. The Japanese know this. It's one reason for their economic success. Living in a land poor in natural resources, they covet human resources. Businesses that are fortunate in their employees are usually fortunate in business. In a culture of action leadership, there cannot be a more important accomplishment than recruiting and retaining motivated people. Even the goal of fulfilling customer needs cannot be made more important. For without motivated people, a company cannot best fulfill customer needs.

challenging interview

Avoid hiring people simply because of the knowledge and/or the degrees they possess. Clearly, it is important that people know, but more important is what they do with what they know. Attitude transforms knowing into doing. Terrific people usually have a terrific attitude. Not-so-terrific people usually lack it. Make a terrific attitude be a key attribute of people you hire. Often, you can only discover attitude, or lack thereof, by challenging them during the interview process, which is an opportunity to communicate your vision, values and expectations.

Think of the interviewee in terms of action leadership. Would she work best under order leadership or action leadership? Frame your questions within the techniques of this book. Does that person wait for opportunity to knock, or does she have a habit of tearing the door off its hinges even before the knock comes? Hire the people who make things happen rather than let them happen. The difference between the let-things-happen people and the make-things-happen people is almost always attitude.

— retire with fire

When people who served well make their departure, insure that the band plays with warm regards and that the banners of respect and appreciation fly, however you define and display a band and banners in your organization. Whether the person is retiring or being hired away, make a heartfelt ceremony of the leaving. Always give a heartfelt speech. Make it a true motivational speech by hitting the need/belief/action keys.

fair-weather sincerity

Likewise, when people are fired or laid off, invest their departure with dignity and compassion. If a goal of action leadership is to establish sincere relationships with people, then those relationships must extend even to those in the organization whose leaving is not under the best of circumstances. Otherwise, your sincerity may be viewed as only a fair-weather kind.

'they were shamed!'

A middle-aged banking executive told me of the time she was fired as a loan officer at a bank in a Midwestern town. She and the department she headed had consistently stayed within the budget and achieved their financial targets, but a merger of her bank with a much larger bank led to an influx of new management who undertook a cost-cutting frenzy. They fired her and hired a replacement 15 years younger at half her salary. "Getting fired for no good reason other than the fact that my salary was too high was distressing enough," she said, "But the worst thing was the way they did it. I was told out of the blue over the phone by the assistant to the human-resources director. And if that wasn't bad enough, a policeman was hired to come in and stand over my desk while I cleaned it out to make sure that I wasn't stealing anything. You know who that policeman was? He was the town's chief of police. I had grown up in that town. I had known the chief for years. Apparently, the bank's spare guard was on another assignment, so they subcontracted the local police to do the job, and the chief was the only officer available. He was embarrassed. I was embarrassed. What an awful, awful scene! That happened a few years ago, and it still pains me to think about it. But you know what I've come to learn from that? *I* wasn't shamed by the way I was let go. *They* were the ones who were shamed."

a time for courtesy

When people are to be let go, be the messenger. Give people the dignity of speaking face-to-face with you. "Life is not so short," said Emerson, "that there is always time for courtesy."

Also, visit them, be there with them, in their humiliation. The battalion commander I mentioned in the previous chapter constantly visited his troops who were in the brig. "Even though they are in the brig," he said, "They're still Marines and still need and deserve my attention."

— make people coaches

When people feel left out of the picture, they get demoralized and demotivated. Create a culture in which the participants believe that they are a central part of the picture, not on its fringe. Treat them as if they are player/coaches, people who direct the action while being in the action. Whatever position people have in an organization, they should be made to feel that they and the position they hold are vital to that organization's success and that their coaching contributes to that success. These messages must be reinforced by your continually doing two things: First, you are there telling and showing them how their team is important; and second, you are encouraging them to coach others on the team. In that way, you are re-enforcing vision and stimulating people to develop leadership skills.

truly important teams

Everybody, even people in the lowest entry-level positions, should see themselves as player/coaches. Encourage them to get involved in other people's jobs. In order-leadership culture, which is often characterized by clearly delineated and vigorously defended turf, people are expected to be put in their place and stay in their place. But in an action-leadership culture, people are encouraged to put themselves in other people's places.

innovation through non-expertise

Great advances in innovation often occur when people who are expert in one field enter another field in which they know little. Expertise can inhibit innovation. Experts usually have an excessive confidence in their knowledge. Many times, people who have such confidence are ill-suited to make bold discoveries. Author Arthur C. Clarke said, "When a distinguished but elderly scientist states that something is possible, he is almost certainly right. When he states that something is impossible, he is almost certainly wrong." The first synthetic dye was produced not by a chemist but by an 18-year-old English schoolboy in 1856 who had been trying to develop synthetic quinine. King Gillette said that if he was technically trained, he never would have invented the safety razor. Marine biologist Rachel Carson didn't just enter a new field, she actually created one, environmental science, by alerting the public to the dangers of pollution in her book *Silent Spring*. Great advances in your business can take place when people are encouraged to be cross-job player/coaches.

pinstripes and lab coats

However, these endeavors may prove destructive to an organization if not supported by a culture that doesn't just tolerate but cherishes them. A marketing director should welcome a shipping clerk's suggestions that the products are not properly packaged. A CEO should welcome an assembly-line worker's recommendation on sales strategy. Pinstripes should welcome lab coats' advice, and lab coats welcome pinstripes' advice. In an action-leadership culture in which everyone is a player/coach and accepts others as being player/coaches, breaching the impregnable and doing the impossible are activities that fall within the realm of the possible.

— use repetition

The most effective radio and television commercials are often not the entertaining ones but the ones that keep repeating the names of the products. For your culture's vision and values to be replicated, they must be repeated many times in many ways. Many leaders have told me, "I don't want to keep repeating myself. If I get sick of hearing myself say the same thing again and again, think of how my listeners feel!" Let's disenthrall ourselves of such ideas. We may not like constantly communicating the same values and vision, but without such communication, our culture could not flourish.

it's right when you're sick of it

The people with whom you work closely must recognize this as well. A staff person of a CEO once told me, "He's driving me nuts always repeating the same thing. He talks about 'consensus leadership' over and over again. Why doesn't he get on another kick?"

I replied, "When you're tired of listening, he's doing it right, not wrong! If an executive's staff *isn't* sick of hearing the message again and again, that executive is a poor communicator."

pizza and vision

Another CEO said, "I grew up poor, and my mother found a trillion ways to make pizza. Communicating your vision and values over and over again is like making pizza taste different every time you have it."

a yard of tape

We make a living by what we get and also what we give. Our work should justify and enrich our existence. The culture of action leadership begins in the individual heart of each leader but finds meaning in work and in the actions of others. Emerson said, "If we weave a yard of tape in all humility and as well as we can, long hereafter, we shall see it was no cotton tape at all but some galaxy which we braided, and that the threads were time and nature." When motivating people to take action, there are many ways to meet a payroll.

INDEX

ABOUT THE AUTHOR

Brent Filson first learned about leadership communication as a Marine Corps infantry officer. Since then, he has published 16 books on a variety of subjects, from physics to phobias, and more than 100 magazine articles. His books have sold more than a million copies. As president of Brent Filson Communications, he has worked with major companies in the United States and Europe, developing communication strategies, in-house training programs, writing speeches and giving lectures and seminars. He and his book, *Executive Speeches*, have been featured in more than 100 magazines and newspapers, and he has been interviewed on several hundred radio and television programs. A graduate of Wake Forest University, he lives in the Massachusetts Berkshires with his wife and children.